Welcome! This book was made for anyone who wants to start sewing — no experience needed. Every project includes a flat pattern diagram with measurements and step-by-step instructions written as clearly as possible.

Table of Contents

Must Read 4-6

Basic sewing tools / Needed hand stitches 4

Helpful presser feet / Seam allowance and hemming / Fabric ... 5

Fabric estimation 6

Pin Cushion 8

Chapter 1: Kitchen Accessories 10-31

Waist Apron 11

Victorian Apron 14

Chef's Apron & Hat 17-20

Kid's Apron & Chef Hat 21

Heart Pot Holders 24

Oven Mitts & Mini Mitts 26

Business Ideas 31

Chapter 2: Hair & Beauty 32-56

Scrunchies 33

Hair Bows 36

Heatless Hair Curler 39

Twisted Headband 41

Hair Towel Wrap 43

Satin Hair Bonnet 45

Cottagecore Bandana 47

Sleeping Eye Mask 49

Reusable Makeup Pads 51

Exfoliating Body Gloves 53

Business Ideas 55

Chapter 3: Home Decor 57-72

Fitted Bedsheets 58

Envelope Pillowcase 61

Travel Neck Pillow 64

Bean Bag Chair 67

Bolster Pillowcase 69

Business Ideas 71

Chapter 4: Bags 73-88

Tote Bag 74

Toiletry Bag 76

Puffer Bag 78

Shoulder Bag 81

Bottle Bag 83

Lunch Bag 85

Business Ideas 88

Chapter 5: Baby Accessories 89-101

Bucket Hat 90

Baby Play Mat 93

Baby Bib / Burp Cloth 95

Baby Bloomers 97

Baby Sleeping Bag 99

Business Ideas 101

About the Author 102

Basic Sewing Tools:
- **Scissors:** Use fabric scissors only for cutting fabric — using them on paper will dull the blade quickly. Keep a separate pair for paper patterns.
- **Measuring tape:** A flexible tape used to take body measurements and measure fabric. Essential for every project in this book.
- **Pins and needles:** Pins hold your fabric pieces together before sewing. Hand sewing needles are used for finishing stitches like the invisible stitch.
- **Tailor's chalk, water-soluble pens, or fabric markers:** Used to mark measurements and lines directly on fabric. All marks disappear either by washing or with heat. A great option is the Frixion erasable ink pen — the marks vanish completely when you press them with a hot iron.
- **Seam Ripper:** A small tool used to remove stitches when you make a mistake. Every sewist needs one — don't be afraid to use it!
- **Iron and Ironing Board:** Pressing your fabric before, during, and after sewing makes a huge difference in the final result. Never skip ironing.
- **Craft paper or any large paper:** Used to draft your pattern pieces before cutting into fabric. Old newspaper or parchment paper works perfectly.
- **Rotary Cutter and Cutting Mat:** A cutting mat is a self-healing mat that protects your table. A rotary cutter is a round-bladed rolling tool that cuts fabric cleanly and is especially useful for cutting curves. Neither is essential but both make cutting faster and more accurate.
- **Loop Turner:** A long thin metal tool with a small hook at one end. You insert it into a sewn fabric tube, hook the fabric at the far end, and pull it back through to turn the tube right side out. Very useful for straps, ties, and handles.

Important: Always start and end every seam with a backstitch — sew 3–4 stitches forward, then 3–4 stitches backward, then continue forward. This locks your thread in place and prevents your seam from unraveling over time.

Needed Hand Stitches:
- **Basting stitch:** A long, loose temporary stitch used to hold fabric pieces together before final sewing, or to create gathers by pulling the thread. It is always removed after the final stitch is sewn.

- **Invisible stitch (also called ladder stitch):** Used to close an opening by hand so the stitches are completely hidden. Fold both fabric edges inward so all raw edges are tucked inside. Bring your needle up through the fold on one side, then cross directly over and pick up a small stitch from the fold on the opposite side. Continue alternating sides, keeping your stitches small and even. Repeat until the opening is fully closed. Pull the thread gently — the gap closes and the stitches disappear. Finish with a secure knot hidden between the folds.

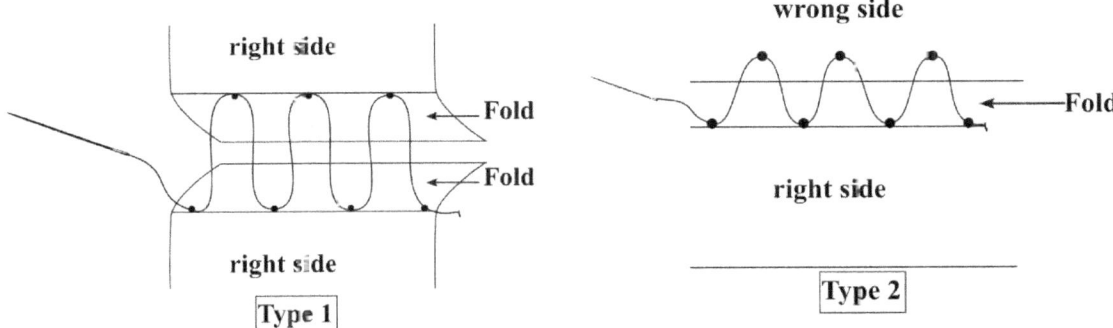

- **Helpful Presser Feet:**
- **Zipper Foot:** A narrow foot that lets you sew very close to a zipper coil or piping cord. Used whenever a project includes a zipper or piped edge.
- **Walking Foot:** Feeds multiple layers of fabric through the machine evenly at the same time. Ideal for quilting, sewing thick fabrics, or working with tricky materials like vinyl, leather, or knit.
- **Rolled Hem Foot:** Automatically folds and sews a very narrow, clean hem in one pass. Especially useful for lightweight fabrics like chiffon or satin. Without it, you would need to fold and iron a tiny hem by hand before sewing.
- **Overcast Foot:** Sews over the raw edge of fabric to prevent fraying, mimicking what a serger does. Very useful if you don't own an overlock machine.
- **Gathering Foot:** Automatically creates evenly distributed gathers or ruffles as you sew. Saves a lot of time compared to gathering by hand.

Seam Allowance and Hemming:

- **Seam allowance:** When you sew two pieces of fabric together, you don't sew right at the raw edge — you sew a small distance inward. That strip of fabric between the raw edge and your stitch line is the seam allowance. In this book, all seam allowances are **1 cm** unless a project states otherwise. Most sewing machines have measurement markings on the needle plate to help you keep a consistent distance.
- **Hemming:** Hemming means folding a raw edge over — usually twice — so the raw edge is completely hidden, then sewing it down. The first fold is typically 0.5 cm and the second fold is 1 cm. Always press your folds with an iron before sewing for a clean, professional result.

Fabric:

- **Lengthwise Grain (Warp):** Runs parallel to the selvage — the finished edge of the fabric. This is the strongest, least stretchy direction. Most pattern pieces are placed along the lengthwise grain for the best result.
- **Crosswise Grain (Weft):** Runs perpendicular to the selvage, from one side of the fabric to the other. It has slightly more stretch than the lengthwise grain, which is why some waistbands and ruffles are cut in this direction.

- **Bias:** The diagonal direction, at a 45-degree angle to both grains. Fabric cut on the bias has the most stretch and drape, making it ideal for binding, curved edges, and flowing garments.
- **Selvage:** The tightly woven finished edge that runs along both long sides of the fabric. It does not fray and is used as a reference to identify the grain direction. Never include the selvage in your project — always cut it off.
- **Nap:** Refers to the surface texture of certain fabrics that runs in one direction, like velvet, fleece, or corduroy. When you run your hand one way it feels smooth, and the other way it feels rough. When cutting fabric with a nap, always make sure every pattern piece is placed facing the same direction — otherwise your finished project will look like two different shades.

Fabric Estimation:

Estimating how much fabric to buy before starting a project is one of the most useful sewing skills. Here is a simple method:

Look at the diagram page for your project and note all the pattern pieces and their measurements. On a large piece of paper, draw a rectangle that is 150 cm wide — this represents a standard fabric width. Arrange all your pattern pieces inside this rectangle as efficiently as possible, fitting them side by side like a puzzle. The total length of the rectangle you filled is roughly how much fabric you need to buy. Always add an extra 10–15 cm as a buffer for mistakes or re-cuts.

Important: If your fabric has a printed pattern or a nap, all pieces must face the same direction. This means you cannot flip pieces to save space, so buy a little extra.

Tip: When in doubt, buy more than you think you need. Leftover fabric is always useful — running short mid-project is frustrating.

Before starting any project in this book, keep these tips in mind:
- **Read through all the steps first** before cutting a single piece of fabric. This gives you a clear picture of the whole process.
- **Press with your iron as you go** — not just at the end. Ironing each seam as you sew makes a significant difference in the final result.
- **Always backstitch** at the start and end of every seam to lock your stitches in place.
- **Cut slowly and carefully** — a straight, accurate cut saves you a lot of trouble when assembling pieces together.
- **Seam allowance is 1 cm throughout this book** unless a project states otherwise.
- **Don't be discouraged by mistakes** — even experienced sewists use their seam ripper regularly. Unpicking and redoing a seam is completely normal.

Wrist Pincushion

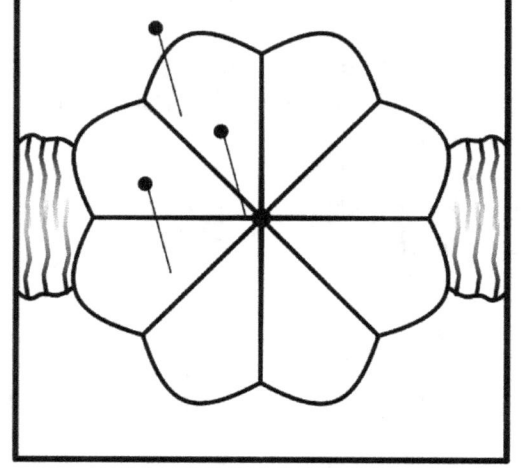

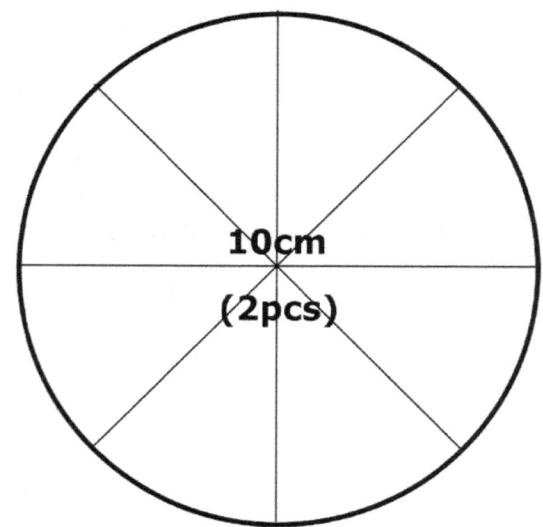

10cm
(2pcs)

wrist×2

Fabric

8cm

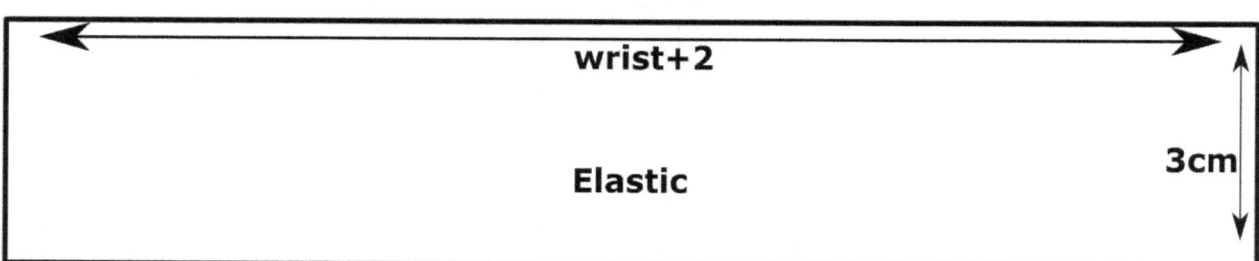

wrist+2

Elastic

3cm

Cm	In
10cm	3.94in
8cm	3.15in
3cm	1.18in

The perfect first project — quick, useful, and a great way to practice before moving on to bigger things.

Materials Needed:
- Scrap fabric of your choice
- Polyester Fiberfill or cotton for stuffing
- Elastic
- Scissors
- Measuring tape
- Tailor's chalk or any marking tool
- Thread and needle
- Hot glue gun (optional)

Instructions:

Step 1: Fold your fabric in half and cut out 2 circles, each 10 cm in diameter. On one circle, use your chalk to draw lines dividing it into 8 equal pie-slice sections — like cutting a pizza into 8 slices. Draw these lines on the right side of the fabric. Do not cut along these lines, they are just guides for later.

Step 2: Measure around your wrist with your measuring tape and write that number down. Cut a rectangle from your fabric that is 8 cm wide and as long as your wrist measurement multiplied by 2. For example, if your wrist measures 16 cm, your rectangle should be 8 cm × 32 cm.

Step 3: Cut your elastic to the same length as your wrist measurement. Make sure the elastic is 3 cm wide.

Step 4a: Place your two circles on top of each other with the right sides facing each other (the pretty sides touching). Sew around the edge with a 1 cm seam allowance, leaving a 4 cm gap unsewn — this is where you will add the stuffing later. Set aside.

Step 4b: Take your rectangle and fold it in half lengthwise with right sides facing each other. Sew along the long raw edge with a 1 cm seam allowance to create a tube. Turn the tube right side out — it should now be 3 cm wide. Insert your elastic through the tube and stitch both ends of the elastic securely to the ends of the tube.

Step 5: Take your sewn circle and clip small notches around the curved edge, being careful not to cut through the stitches — this helps the fabric lie flat when turned. Turn it right side out through the gap. Stuff it firmly with Polyfill or fabric scraps until it feels full and rounded. Close the gap using an invisible stitch.

Step 6: Cut about 1 meter of thick thread and thread your needle with a secure knot at one end. Push the needle through the very center of the stuffed circle from the bottom. Following the chalk lines you drew in Step 1, stitch along each line from the center outward and back, pulling gently to create 8 defined petal sections. When all 8 lines are done, tie a firm knot at the center and trim the excess thread.

Step 7: Attach the stuffed circle to the elastic band. If you have a hot glue gun, glue it in place then secure it further with a few hand stitches around the edge. If you don't have a glue gun, simply stitch the circle directly onto the elastic band all the way around.

Tip: You can make other shapes like hearts or stars using the same method — just change the pattern piece and adjust the division lines accordingly.

Business Ideas: Sell personalized pincushions on local e-commerce platforms and social media. Experiment with different shapes, fabrics, and sizes — sets of matching pincushions make great gifts for sewists!

Chapter 1
Kitchen Accessories

How to take your measurements:

Waist Apron: Wrap your measuring tape around your natural waist (the narrowest part of your torso). That measurement is your waist width. For the length, hold the tape at your waist and let it hang down to where you want the apron to end — measure that distance.

Victorian Apron skirt: Measure your waist as above. To get the gathered skirt width, multiply your waist measurement by 1.5 for light gathers, by 2 for medium gathers, or by 3 for very full, ruffled gathers. The more you multiply, the fuller the skirt will look.

Apron bib and straps: For the bib width, measure across your chest from side to side — just enough to cover the area you want. For the neck strap, place the tape at the front of one shoulder, bring it up and over the back of your neck, and down to the other shoulder. For the waist ties, a length of 80 cm per side is standard and gives enough length to tie a bow at the back.

Chef's Apron: Measure the width of your torso at the widest point you want the apron to cover, and the length from just below your chest down to where you want it to end.

Chef's Hat: Measure around your head at the widest point, keeping the tape slightly loose so it is comfortable. Add 2 cm for the seam allowance (1 cm on each side). If you plan to add Velcro for adjustability, add another 2 cm.

How to make and attach binding and bias tape:

Note: Bias tape and binding are used throughout this book to finish raw edges neatly. You will see them mentioned in several projects. Here is how to make and attach them so you are ready when the time comes.

Making your own binding: Cut a strip of fabric either on the straight grain or on the bias (diagonally). Fold the strip in half lengthwise with wrong sides together and press. Open it flat, then fold each raw edge inward to meet the center crease and press again. Finally fold the strip in half along the original center crease so all raw edges are enclosed inside. Press well. Your binding is ready to use.

Making your own bias tape: Fold your fabric diagonally at a 45-degree angle — this is the bias direction. Cut strips along this diagonal. Fold each long edge inward toward the center and press. Then fold the whole strip in half and press again. The bias direction gives the tape flexibility, making it easy to sew around curves without puckering.

Using pre-made bias tape: Unfold one side of the bias tape and align its raw edge with the raw edge of your fabric, right sides together. Pin or clip in place. Sew along the first fold crease. Fold the bias tape over to the wrong side of the fabric, enclosing the raw edge. Pin and topstitch close to the edge from the right side to finish.

Tip: Bias tape is one of the most beginner-friendly finishing tools — it eliminates the need for a serger and gives your work a professional look.

Waist Apron

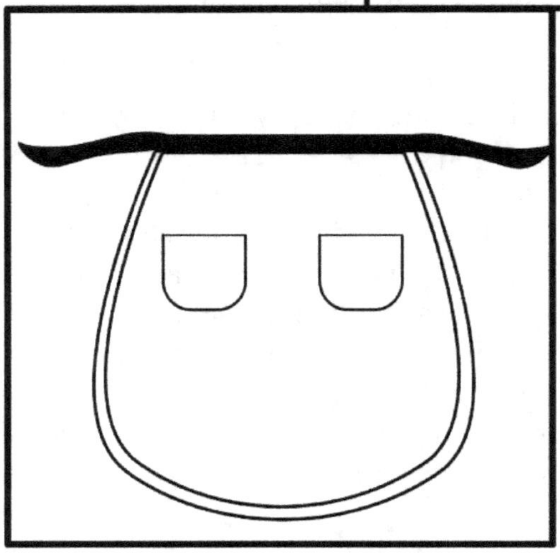

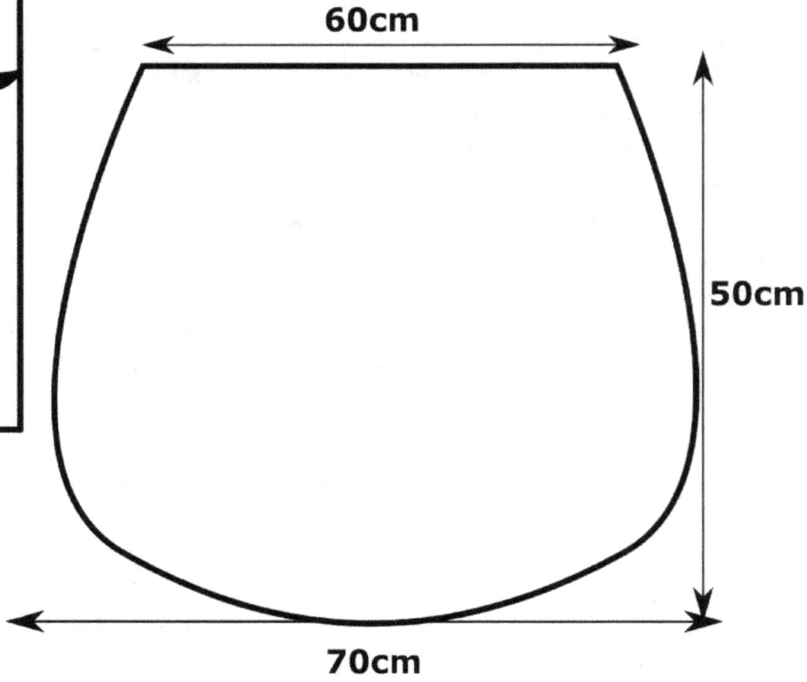

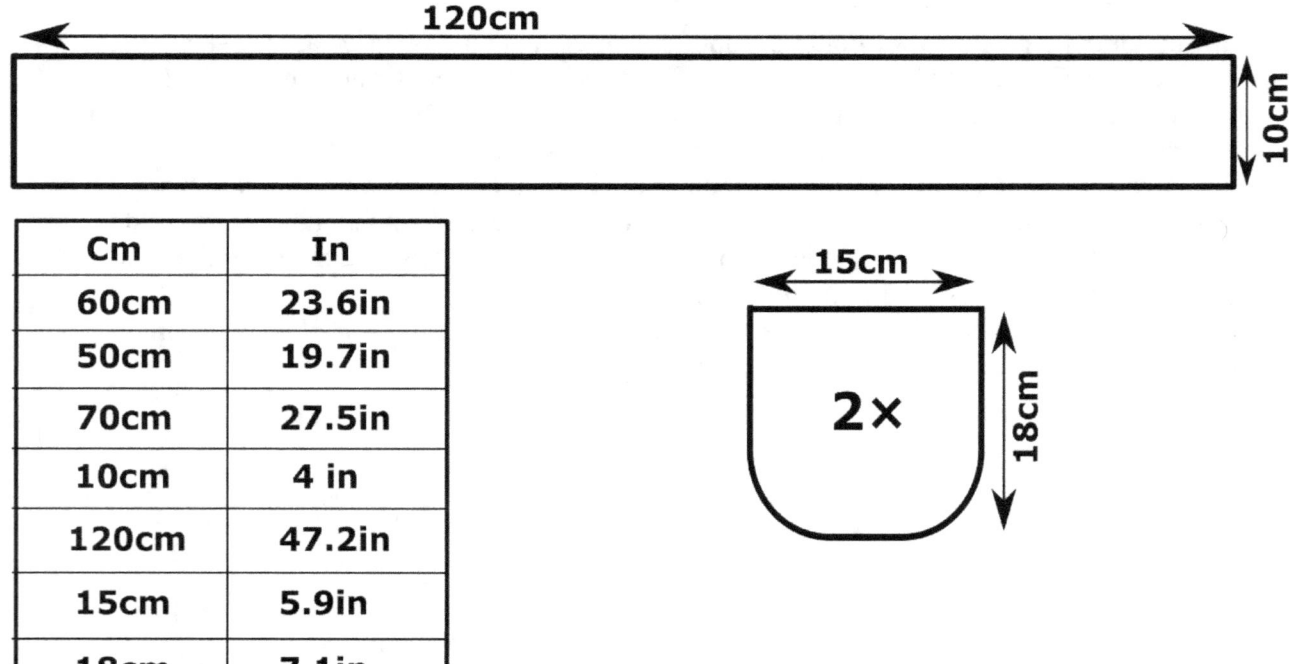

Cm	In
60cm	23.6in
50cm	19.7in
70cm	27.5in
10cm	4 in
120cm	47.2in
15cm	5.9in
18cm	7.1in

Waist Apron

A simple and stylish apron that ties at the waist — perfect for cooking, crafting, or gardening. This is a great beginner project.

Materials Needed:
- 60 cm of fabric
- Bias tape or lace tape (optional)
- Scissors
- Chalk
- Ruler

Instructions:

Step 1: On your fabric, trace a rectangle that is 120 cm wide and 10 cm long. This will be your waist tie. Cut it out.

Step 2: Trace the main apron body: draw a rectangle that is 70 cm wide and 50 cm long. On the top edge, measure 5 cm in from each corner and make a mark — the top edge between these two marks should now measure 60 cm. On the bottom corners, draw a gentle curve to round them slightly, as shown in the diagram. Cut along your traced shape.

Step 3: Fold your fabric in half, then trace a rectangle that is 15 cm wide and 18 cm long. Round the bottom corners slightly. Cut through both layers to get 2 pocket pieces.

Step 4: Take the main apron piece. Fold the right, left, and bottom raw edges to the wrong side by 0.5 cm and press with your iron. Fold them again by 1 cm and press again. This double fold hides the raw edge completely. If you prefer, skip this and attach bias tape along these three edges instead — both give the same clean result.

Step 5: Sew a 1 cm hem along the three folded sides. If you used bias tape, attach it to the three sides and sew in place.

Step 6: Take your waist tie rectangle. Fold the top and bottom long edges inward by 1 cm each and press. You should now have a strip that is 8 cm wide. Fold the whole strip in half lengthwise and press again — your finished waist tie should measure 120 cm × 4 cm. Topstitch along the open long edge to close it.

Step 7: Take your two pocket pieces. Fold and press 1 cm to the wrong side on all four sides. Sew across the top edge of each pocket only.

Step 8: Fold your apron in half vertically and mark the center of the top edge with a pin. Do the same with your waist tie. These center marks will help you attach everything evenly.

Step 9: Lay your waist tie flat. Align its center mark with the center mark on the apron's top edge, with the wrong side of the tie facing the right side of the apron. Sew 1 cm from the top edge of the apron. Now fold the waist tie over to the right side, enclosing the raw edge, and topstitch 2 mm from the edge all the way across.

Step 10: Place the pockets on the apron wherever you like and sew 2 mm from the edge along the right, left, and bottom sides of each pocket. Leave the top open.

Notice: If you didn't use bias tape in Step 4, you can finish the look by sewing lace tape along the sides of the apron — this is completely optional but gives a beautiful decorative finish.

Victorian Apron

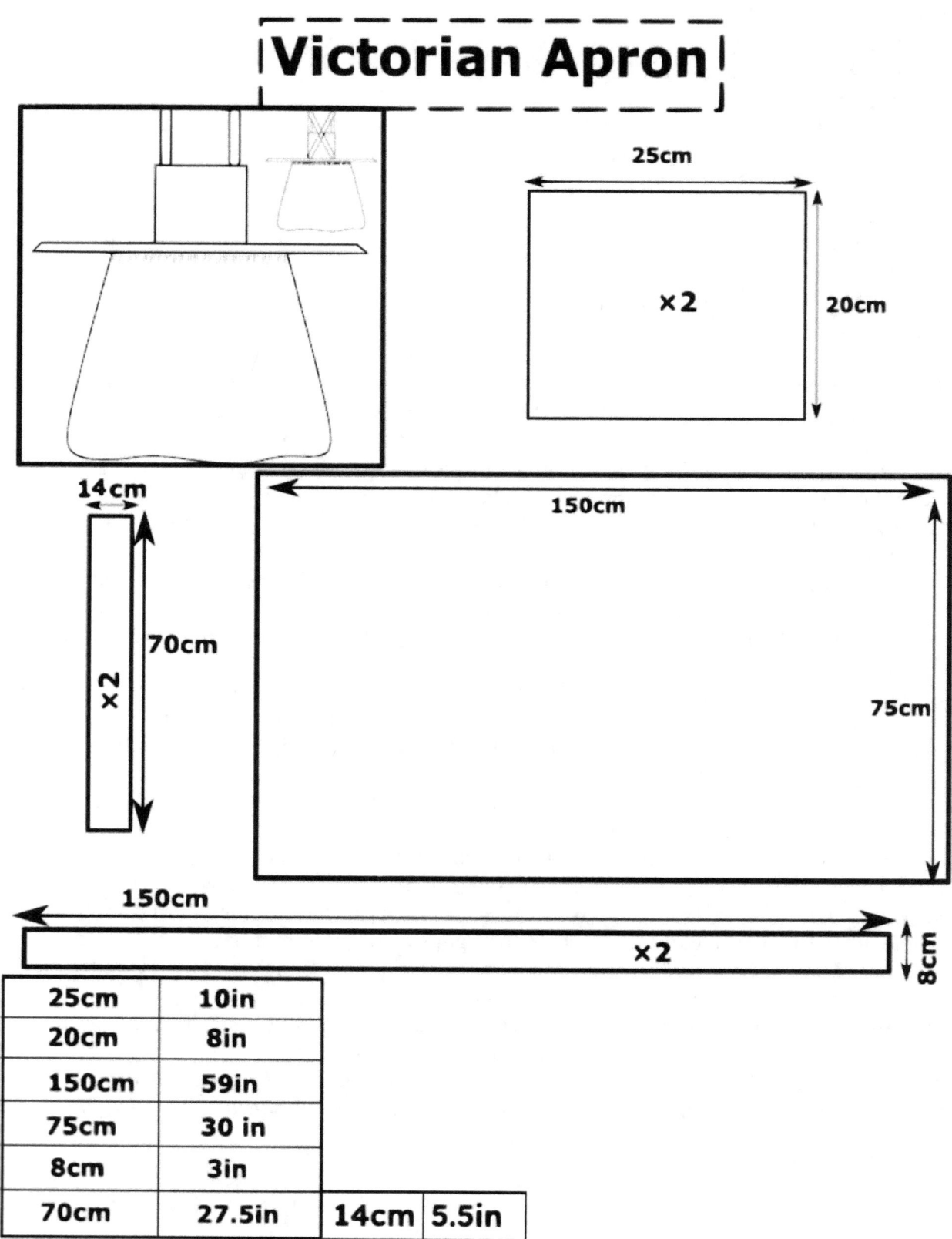

25cm	10in
20cm	8in
150cm	59in
75cm	30 in
8cm	3in
70cm	27.5in

14cm	5.5in

Victorian Apron
A beautiful, full-skirted apron with a gathered skirt, bib, and shoulder straps — elegant and practical at the same time.
Note: The bib is the upper chest piece that sits above the waistband. The waistband wraps around your waist and holds everything together.

Materials Needed:
- 150 to 200 cm of fabric (1.5 to 2 meters)
- Chalk
- Ruler
- Scissors
- Needle and thread

Instructions:
Step 1: Trace and cut a rectangle that is 150 cm wide and 75 cm long. This large piece will be your skirt.

Step 2: Cut two rectangles that are 150 cm wide and 8 cm long. These will be your waistband — one piece is the facing and one is the lining.

Step 3: Trace and cut two rectangles that are 70 cm long and 14 cm wide. These will be your shoulder straps.

Step 4: Fold your fabric in half and trace one rectangle that is 25 cm wide and 20 cm long. Cut through both layers at once to get 2 identical bib pieces.

Step 5: Take your skirt piece and sew a rolled hem along the right, left, and bottom edges. Leave the top edge raw — this is where the gathers will go.

Step 6: On the top edge of your skirt, create gathers until the width reduces to 70 cm. You can do this using one of three methods:
- **Machine method:** Set your sewing machine to its longest stitch length. Sew two parallel lines across the top of the skirt — one 0.5 cm from the edge and one 1 cm from the edge. Do not backstitch at either end. Tie a knot in the threads at one end, then gently pull the loose threads from the other end until the skirt gathers to 70 cm. Distribute the gathers evenly.
- **Hand method:** Sew a long basting stitch by hand across the top edge, then pull the thread slowly to gather the fabric to 70 cm.
- **Gathering foot:** If you have a gathering presser foot, attach it to your machine and sew across the top edge — it will automatically create even gathers.

Step 7: Take your two strap pieces. Place them on top of each other with right sides facing. Sew a 1 cm seam along both long edges and one short end. Trim the corners, flip the strap right side out using a loop turner or pencil, and press flat. Repeat for the second strap.

Step 8: Take both bib pieces. Iron 1 cm to the wrong side on the top, left, and right edges of each piece. Place them on top of each other with right sides facing. Sew the left and right sides following your iron crease. Flip the bib right side out and press well. Leave the bottom edge open and raw.

Step 9: Take your two waistband rectangles. On each one, fold the two short ends into a diagonal point like the tip of a bookmark and press. Then iron 1 cm inward on all four sides of each rectangle, folding toward the wrong side.

Step 10: Place one waistband rectangle on top of the other with right sides facing each other. Sew a 1 cm seam on one short end only, stopping about 5 cm from that end to leave a small opening. Do not sew the rest of the waistband yet — you need to insert the skirt first.

(continued on next page →)

Step 11: Slide your gathered skirt between the two waistband layers, centering it so the skirt sits exactly in the middle. The right side of the skirt should face the lining layer of the waistband. Pin everything in place, then sew along the bottom edge of the waistband through all layers with a 1 cm seam.

Step 12: Take your bib and insert its bottom raw edge between the two waistband layers at the center front, tucking it in about 1 cm. Pin in place and sew a 1 cm seam along the bottom edge of the waistband to secure the bib.

Step 13: Take your straps and insert one end of each strap between the lining and the bib at the top corners of the bib, tucking them in about 1 cm. Pin in place and sew about 3 mm from the top, right, and left edges of the bib to secure the straps.

Step 14: Take the other end of each strap and attach them to the back of the waistband — they should sit right at the point where the skirt begins on each side, tucked between the waistband layers on top of the lining. Sew a 1 cm seam to secure.

Step 15: Pin the two waistband layers together all the way along and topstitch 3 mm from the edge along all sides to close and finish the waistband completely.

Chef's Apron

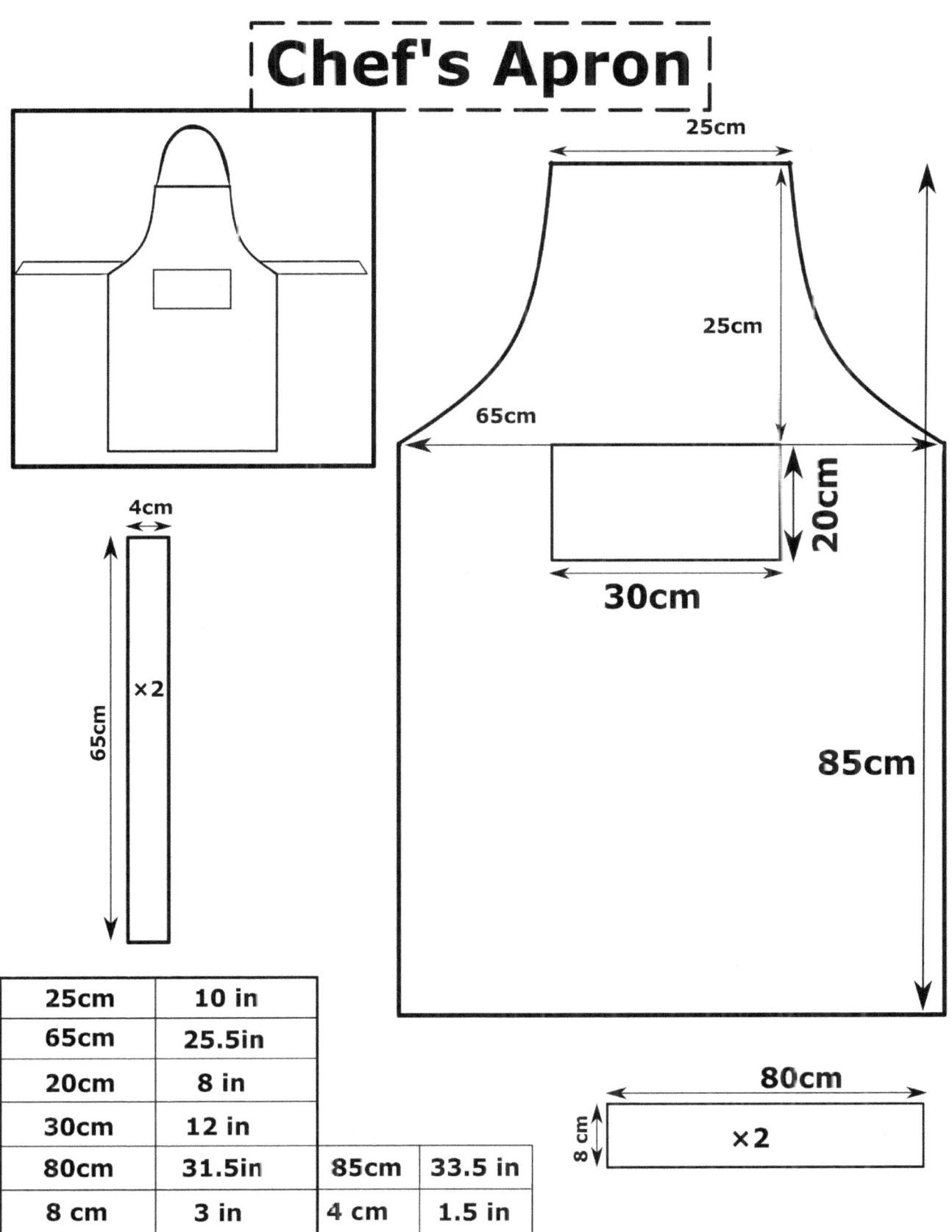

25cm	10 in
65cm	25.5in
20cm	8 in
30cm	12 in
80cm	31.5in
8 cm	3 in

85cm	33.5 in
4 cm	1.5 in

Chef's Apron

A classic full-length apron with a neck strap, waist ties, and a front pocket — the kind you see in professional kitchens.

Materials Needed:
- 1 meter of fabric of your choice
- Chalk
- Ruler
- Scissors

Instructions:

Step 1: On your fabric, trace a rectangle that is 65 cm wide and 85 cm long. This is your main apron body. On the top edge, find the center point and measure 12.5 cm to the left and 12.5 cm to the right — mark both points. The distance between these two marks should be 25 cm and they should sit symmetrically in the middle of the top edge.

Step 2: From the top edge, measure 25 cm downward and draw a horizontal line across the full width of the rectangle. This line marks your waistline.

Step 3: Now connect each of the two marks on the top edge to the corresponding corner of your waistline using a smooth, gently curved line — like a very slight S-curve, not a sharp angle. This creates the armhole cutout shape on each side of the bib. Cut along all your traced lines to get your main apron piece.

Step 4: For the neck strap, trace and cut two rectangles that are 65 cm long and 4 cm wide.

Step 5: For the waist ties, trace and cut two rectangles that are 80 cm wide and 8 cm long.

Step 6: For the pocket, trace and cut one rectangle that is 30 cm wide and 20 cm long.

Step 7: Take your main apron piece and fold all four raw edges 0.5 cm to the wrong side and press. Fold them again 1 cm and press again. Sew a hem along all four sides. Alternatively, use bias tape along the sides for a more polished finish — either purchase it ready-made or make it from leftover fabric as shown on page 11.

Step 8: Take your two neck strap pieces and place them on top of each other with right sides facing. Sew a 1 cm seam along both long edges and one short end. Trim the corners, flip the strap right side out and press flat. Tuck the open end in by 1 cm and press.

Step 9: For each waist tie, take one rectangle and fold it in half lengthwise with right sides facing each other and press. On one short end, fold the corner diagonally to create a pointed tip as shown in the diagram. Sew a 1 cm seam along the long open edge and around the pointed end. Trim the point close to the seam, then flip the tie right side out. Push the pointed tip out fully using a pencil or loop turner. Press flat, fold the open end inward 1 cm, and topstitch 2 mm from the edge along all sides. Repeat for the second waist tie.

Step 10: Repeat the same process for the neck strap — fold the open end inward, press, and topstitch along all sides.

Step 11: Attach the neck strap to the back of the apron at the top of the bib on both sides. Pin in place and sew securely.

Step 12: Attach the waist ties to the sides of the apron at the waistline — the horizontal line you traced in Step 2. Pin them to the wrong side of the apron and sew securely.

Step 13: Take your pocket piece and fold all four edges 1 cm to the wrong side and press. Sew across the top edge only to finish it. Place the pocket on the front of the apron just below the waistline, wherever you like. Pin in place and sew 3 mm from the edge along the right, left, and bottom sides. Leave the top open.

Chef's Hat

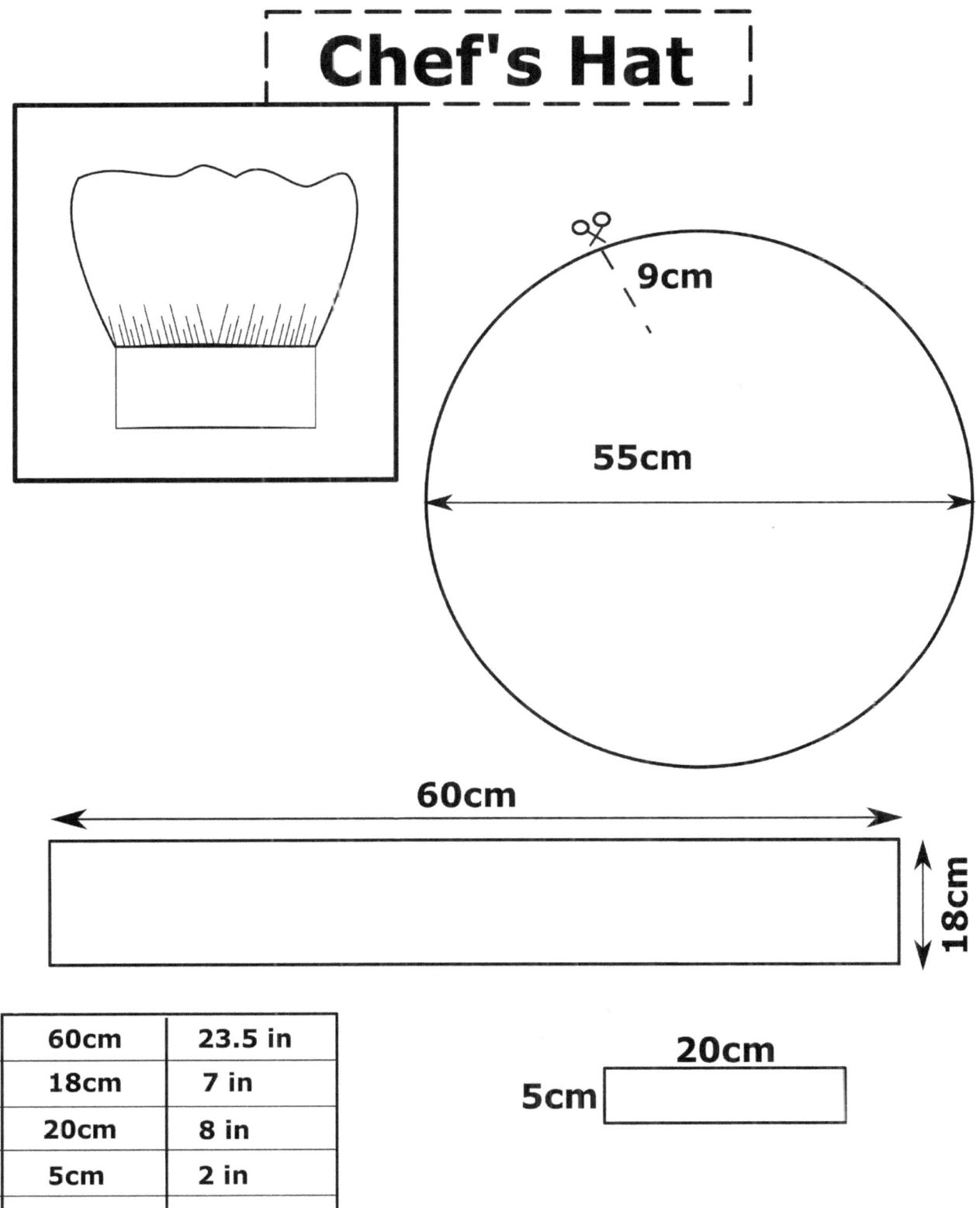

60cm	23.5 in
18cm	7 in
20cm	8 in
5cm	2 in
55cm	22 in
9cm	3.5 in

Chef's Hat
A classic tall chef's hat that is fully adjustable thanks to Velcro. Made with just three pieces of fabric.

Materials Needed:
- 3/4 meter of thick fabric
- Chalk
- Ruler
- Scissors
- 12 cm of Velcro
- Bias tape (optional)

Instructions:

Step 1: Trace a circle with a diameter of 55 cm on the wrong side of your fabric and cut it out. This is the top of your hat. On the edge of the circle, make a straight cut of 9 cm going toward the center — this slit is where the band will be inserted later.

Step 2: Cut a rectangle that is 60 cm wide and 18 cm long. This will be your hat band. You can cut it up to 64 cm wide for a larger head size.

Step 3: Cut a small rectangle that is 5 cm wide and 20 cm long, cutting it on the bias direction of your fabric — diagonally at a 45-degree angle as shown in the diagram. This piece will be used to bind the slit on your circle. Skip this step if you already have bias tape.

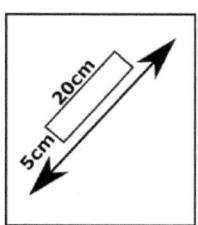

Step 4: On the top edge of your circle, sew a running stitch or set your machine to the longest stitch length and sew all the way around the circle. Gently pull the thread to gather the circle until its circumference measures 58 cm. Distribute the gathers evenly — you can make them random, uniform, or even folded as pleats depending on your preference.

Step 5: Take your large band rectangle and fold it in half lengthwise with wrong sides together and press well. Open it flat, then fold each long raw edge inward by 1 cm toward the center crease and press. Fold it in half again along the original crease — you should now have a neat band that is 58 cm wide and 8 cm tall with all raw edges hidden inside.

Step 6: Take your small bias rectangle (or ready-made bias tape). Fold and press it to make bias tape as explained on page 11. Sew this bias tape along both edges of the 9 cm slit on your circle to finish the raw edges neatly and prevent fraying.

Step 7: Sew the bias tape firmly along the slit of your circle, enclosing both raw edges of the slit inside the tape.

Step 8: Open your band flat. Find the center crease line — this is the fold line from Step 5. Place your Velcro pieces 1 cm away from each short end of the band, on opposite sides — the soft side on one end and the rough side on the other end, so they can fasten together when the band is wrapped around your head. Sew all four sides of each Velcro piece to secure.

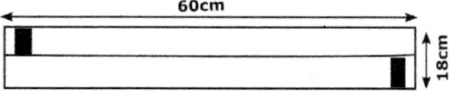

Step 9: Fold the band again along its center crease. Insert the gathered edge of your circle into the band about 1 cm, centering the slit at one end of the band. Pin all the way around and topstitch along the top, left, and right sides of the band to close it and secure the circle inside.

kid's chef hat

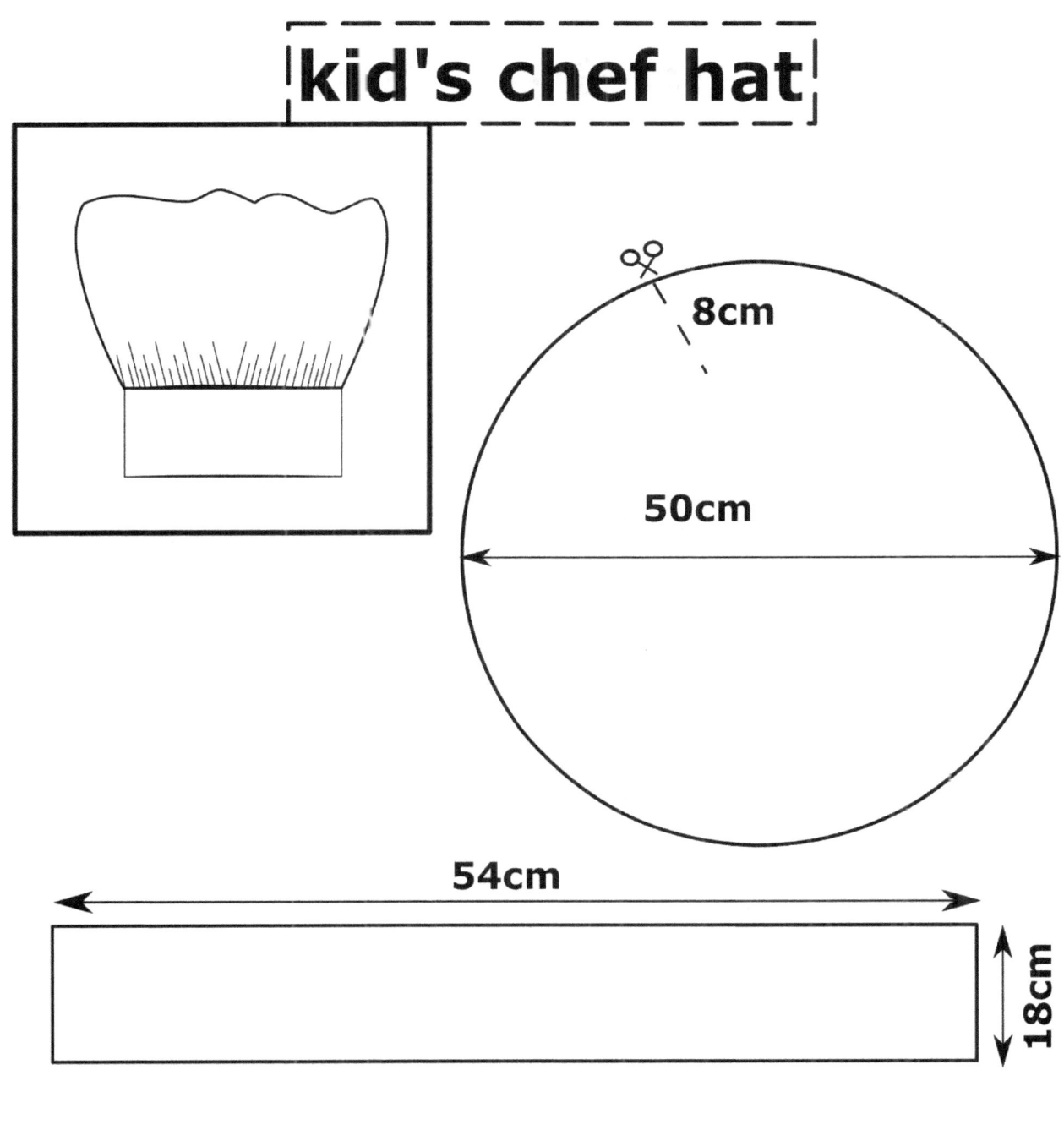

50cm	20 in
8cm	3 in
54cm	21.5 in
18cm	7 in
5cm	2 in

kid's Apron

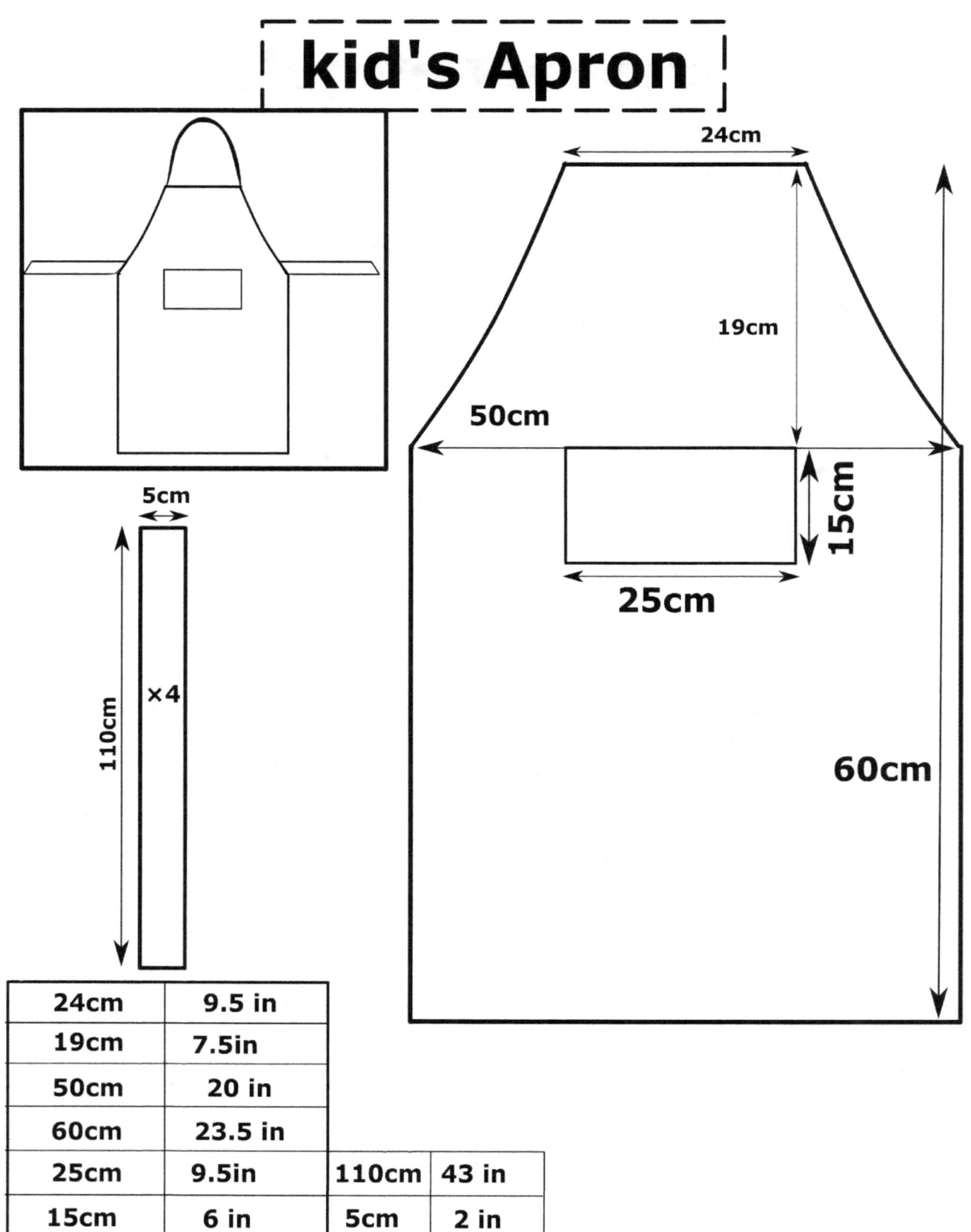

24cm	9.5 in		
19cm	7.5in		
50cm	20 in		
60cm	23.5 in		
25cm	9.5in	110cm	43 in
15cm	6 in	5cm	2 in

Kid's Chef Hat
Follow the exact same steps as the Adult Chef's Hat on page 20 — only the measurements are different, as shown in the diagram on page 21.

Kid's Apron
A fun, easy-to-wear apron for little chefs and artists. The straps slide through casings on the sides — no tying needed, making it perfect for kids.

Materials Needed:
- 3/4 meter of fabric
- Chalk
- Ruler
- Scissors
- Bias tape (optional)

Instructions:
Step 1: On your fabric, trace a rectangle that is 50 cm wide and 60 cm long. On the top edge, measure 13 cm in from each corner and mark a point. From each mark, draw a straight diagonal line down toward the bottom — about 19 cm long. These diagonal lines are your armhole edges. Cut along all traced lines.

Step 2: Sew a rolled hem along all edges except the two diagonal armhole lines. You can use bias tape on those edges instead if you prefer.

Step 3: Take each diagonal armhole edge and fold it inward by 0.5 cm and press. Fold inward again by 2.5 cm and press. Topstitch close to the inner folded edge to create a casing — this is the tunnel your strap will slide through later. Repeat on both sides.

Step 4: Cut four strap rectangles each 5 cm wide and 110 cm long. Sew two rectangles end to end with a 1 cm seam to make one long strap of about 218 cm. Press the seam flat. Repeat with the other two rectangles for the second strap.

Step 5: Press all four edges of each strap inward by 1 cm, folding the short ends in neatly. Fold the whole strap in half lengthwise, press well, and topstitch 2 mm from the edge along all sides.

Step 6: Place one strap on top of the other, aligning them perfectly, and topstitch along both long sides to join them into one flat double-layered strap.

Step 7: Insert one end of the joined strap into the top casing on one side and pull it through until it comes out of the waist casing on the same side. Repeat on the other side. When worn, the strap crosses over the back and keeps the apron in place without any tying needed.

Note: To make an adjustable adult version using this same design, use the adult Chef's Apron pattern from page 17 and change the top edge width to 30 cm. The strap should measure 245 cm × 2 cm.

Heart Pot Holders

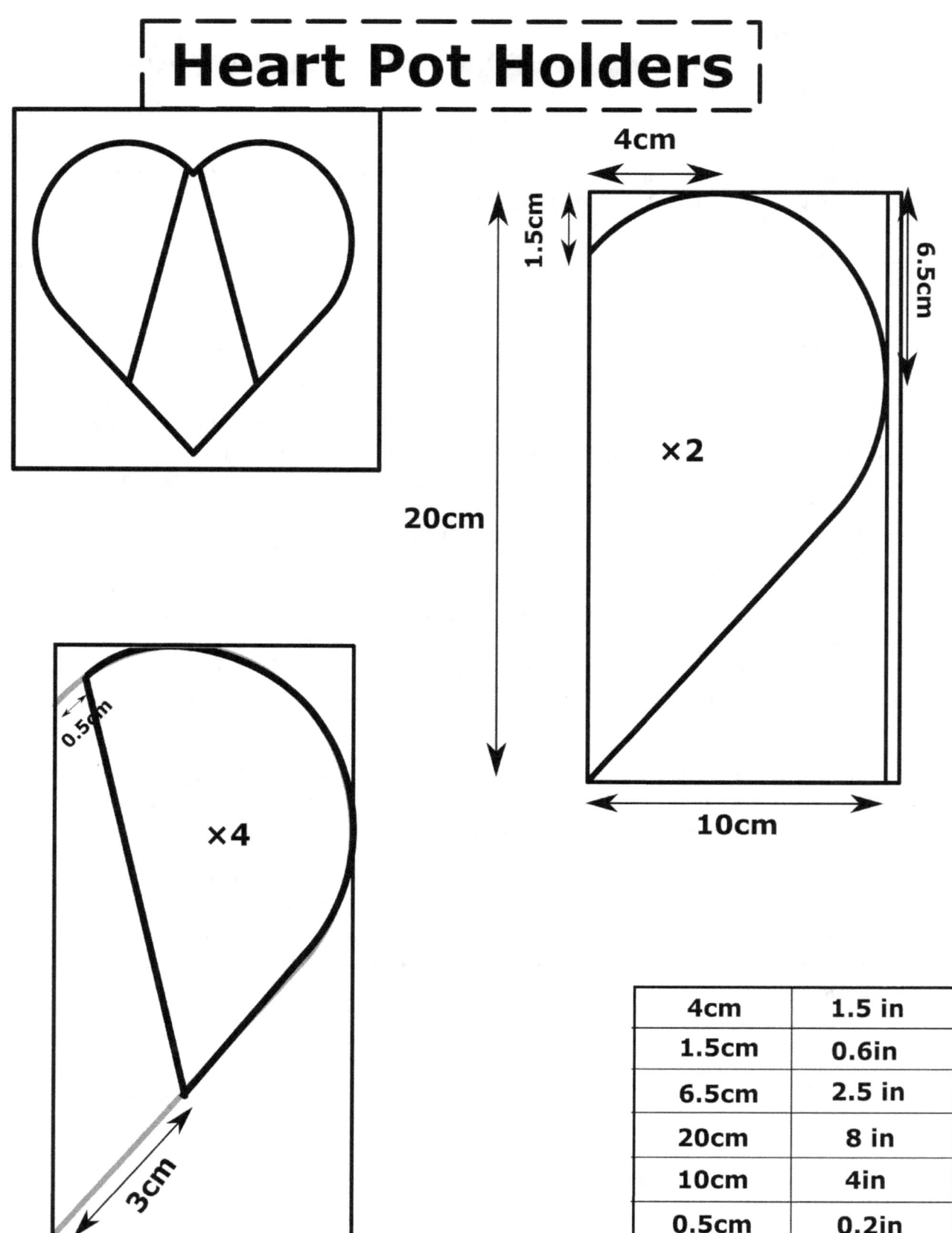

4cm	1.5 in
1.5cm	0.6in
6.5cm	2.5 in
20cm	8 in
10cm	4in
0.5cm	0.2in

Avoid polyester fabric for this project — it is not heat resistant. Cotton, denim, or canvas are all safe choices.

Materials Needed:
- 1/4 meter of cotton fabric
- Thermal batting
- Scissors
- Chalk
- Pins
- Bias tape (optional

Method 1 — Quilt first, then cut:
Step 1: Lay your fabric wrong side up on a flat surface. Place a piece of thermal batting on top of it. Then lay a second piece of fabric on top with the right side facing up. You now have a three-layer sandwich — fabric, batting, fabric.

Step 2: Pin all three layers together so nothing shifts. Sew straight lines across the entire surface, either parallel lines about 2–3 cm apart or random lines in any direction. This is called quilting and it holds all three layers firmly together.

Step 3: Place your heart pattern pieces on top of the quilted fabric, trace around them, and cut them out. You now have quilted, ready-to-use pieces.

Method 2 — Cut first, then quilt:
Step 1: Fold your fabric in half with right sides together. Place your big heart half pattern on top, trace it, and cut through both layers at once — you will get 2 identical big heart halves. Repeat this process to get 2 more big heart halves from a different fabric if you want a contrasting look. You need 4 big heart half pieces total.

Step 2: Using the small heart half pattern, cut 4 small heart half pieces the same way — fold fabric, trace, and cut through both layers.

Step 3: Cut 2 pieces of thermal batting using the big heart half pattern, and 2 more pieces using the small heart half pattern — 4 batting pieces total.

Step 4: For the binding, you can use ready-made bias tape or make your own. You will need two short strips — each measuring 18.5 cm × 5 cm — for the straight edges of the small heart halves. For the long strip that goes all the way around the finished heart, measure around the outer edge of your big heart and add 2 cm extra.

Step 5: Take one big heart half piece with its wrong side facing up. Lay one piece of batting on top, then place the second big heart half piece on top with its right side facing up. You should have: fabric (wrong side up) → batting → fabric (right side up). Pin all layers together and quilt them with straight or random lines. Repeat this process with the other two big heart half pieces and their batting.

Step 6: Repeat the same layering and quilting process for the small heart halves — each small half heart should have one piece of batting sandwiched inside.

Step 7: Take your two short bias strips and sew one along the straight flat edge of each small heart half, enclosing the raw edge neatly inside the bias tape. Topstitch to secure.

Step 8: Place both small heart halves on top of one big quilted heart half, aligning the outer curved edges. The straight bound edges of the small halves should meet in the center forming a V shape — this creates the pocket. Sew all layers together 0.5 cm from the outer curved edge all the way around.

Step 9: Place the second big quilted heart half underneath, wrong sides together, and pin. Take your long bias strip and wrap it all the way around the entire outer edge of the heart, enclosing all raw edges inside. Fold the ends of the bias neatly under at the start and finish point. Topstitch all the way around to secure.

Step 10: Cut a 10 cm strip of bias tape, fold both short ends inward, then fold it in half to make a small loop. Sew it securely to the center top of your heart pot holder — this is the hanging loop.

Oven Mitts

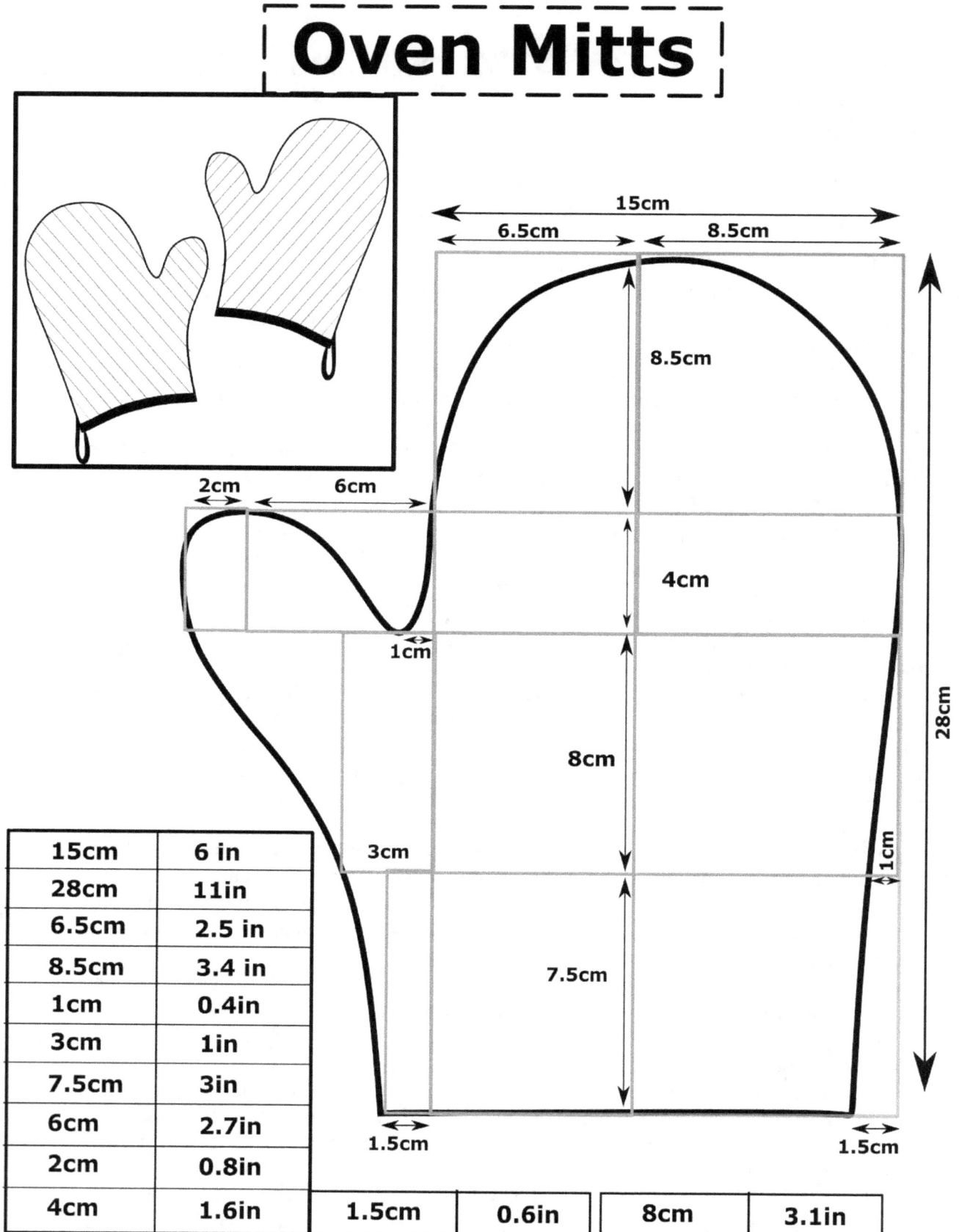

15cm	6 in
28cm	11in
6.5cm	2.5 in
8.5cm	3.4 in
1cm	0.4in
3cm	1in
7.5cm	3in
6cm	2.7in
2cm	0.8in
4cm	1.6in
1.5cm	0.6in
8cm	3.1in

Oven Mitts

A classic pair of quilted oven mitts. Use cotton, denim, or canvas — never polyester, as it is not heat safe. This project uses fusible or thermal batting to protect your hands from heat.

Materials Needed:
- Fabric of your choice (cotton recommended)
- Thermal batting
- Scissors
- Chalk
- Pins
- Bias tape (optional)

Instructions:

Note: To make a custom pattern using your own hand size, place your hand flat on paper, spread your fingers slightly, and trace around it about 4 cm away from your hand on all sides. Round the top into a smooth curve. This is your personal mitt pattern.

Step 1: You will need two pieces of fabric, each about 65 cm × 35 cm — large enough to fit the pattern piece at least twice. If you are using two different fabrics for the inside and outside of the mitts, prepare one piece of each color.

Step 2: Lay one fabric piece on your table with the wrong side facing up. Place two layers of thermal batting on top of it. Then place the second fabric piece on top with its wrong side also facing up — so both fabric pieces have their wrong sides facing outward and the batting is sandwiched in the middle. Pin all layers together and quilt across the whole surface in straight or random lines.

Step 3: Place your pattern on top of the quilted fabric and trace around it. Cut out 4 pieces total. Important: if you want one mitt for the left hand and one for the right, flip your pattern over before cutting 2 of the pieces so they are mirror images of each other.

Step 4: Take two pieces and place them on top of each other with right sides facing inward. Sew around the entire curved edge with a 0.5 cm seam, leaving the straight bottom opening unsewn. Clip small notches around the curves close to the stitching — this helps the mitt keep its shape when turned. Flip inside out and press. Repeat with the remaining two pieces for the second mitt.

Step 5: Take your bias tape and attach it all the way around the raw edge of the bottom opening of each mitt, enclosing the raw edges neatly. Topstitch to secure.

Step 6: To make the hanging loop, take a 10 cm strip of bias tape. Fold both short ends inward by 0.5 cm and press. Fold the strip in half to form a small loop and topstitch 2 mm along the open side to close it. Fold it into a loop and sew it securely to the side seam at the opening of each mitt.

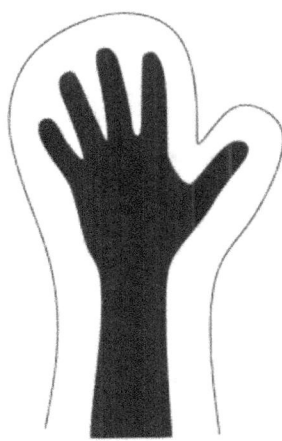

Mini Oven Mitts

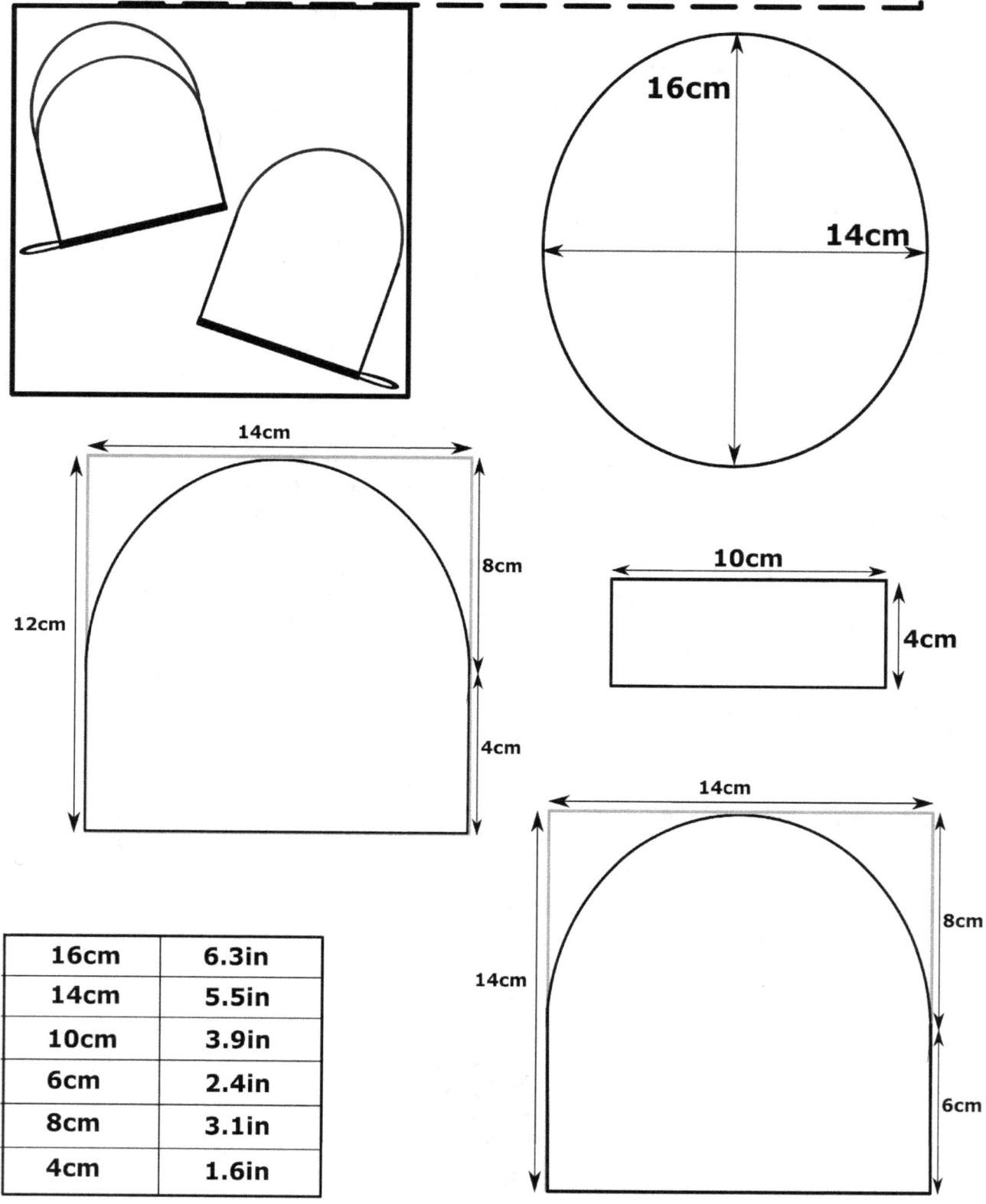

16cm	6.3in
14cm	5.5in
10cm	3.9in
6cm	2.4in
8cm	3.1in
4cm	1.6in

Materials Needed:
- Fabric of your choice
- Fusible batting
- Scissors
- Chalk
- Pins

Instructions:

Step 1: You will be making three pattern pieces from paper. Take a sheet of paper that is 16 cm × 14 cm. Fold it into 4 equal parts. On one corner, draw a smooth curve connecting the two folded edges — like the corner of a rounded rectangle. Cut along the curve through all layers. When you unfold the paper you will have an oval shape. This is Pattern Piece 1.

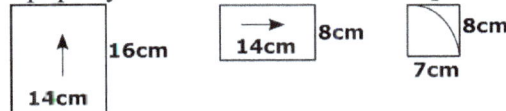

Step 2: Take a second sheet of paper that is 14 cm × 14 cm. Place Pattern Piece 1 (folded in half) on top of it and trace the same curve onto one corner. Cut along the curve — this gives you an arch-shaped piece. This is Pattern Piece 2.

Step 3: Take a third sheet of paper that is 14 cm × 12 cm and repeat the same process to create a slightly smaller arch shape. This is Pattern Piece 3.

You now have 3 pattern pieces — an oval and two different-sized arch pieces.

Step 4: For each of the 3 pattern pieces, cut 2 pieces of batting. You should have 6 batting pieces total.

Step 5: Place each of your 3 pattern pieces on your exterior fabric, adding 1 cm seam allowance on all sides when cutting. Cut 2 fabric pieces for each pattern — 6 exterior fabric pieces total. Repeat this exact process for your lining fabric — 6 lining pieces total.

Step 6: Cut 2 rectangles that are 10 cm × 4 cm from your fabric. These will be your hanging loops.

Step 7: Take all 6 exterior fabric pieces and attach one piece of fusible batting to the wrong side of each. Press with a hot iron to bond them together firmly.

Step 8: Take the largest arch piece (Pattern Piece 2) and the medium arch piece (Pattern Piece 3). Place them on top of each other with right sides facing. Sew a 6 cm line on each side, 1 cm from the edge — start from the bottom straight edge and sew upward 6 cm only. Do not sew the curved top yet. Repeat this with the remaining two arch pieces to make the second mitt exterior.

Step 9: Open your mitt flat so it lies completely open on the table. Place the oval piece (Pattern Piece 1) on top, right sides facing, centering it over the opening. Flip the 6 cm sewn section to one side and sew along one half of the oval. Then flip the sewn section to the other side and sew along the remaining half of the oval. Be careful not to catch the 6 cm stitching in your seam. Turn the mitt right side out through the bottom opening.

Step 10: Repeat Steps 8 and 9 using your lining pieces, but do not turn the lining right side out — leave it inside out.

Step 11: Take your 10 cm × 4 cm hanging loop rectangle. Fold it in half lengthwise with wrong sides together and press. Open it, fold each long edge inward to the center crease and press again. Fold in half once more and topstitch 2 mm along the open side to close. Fold it into a loop.

Step 12: Insert the exterior mitt inside the lining — right sides should be facing each other. Tuck the hanging loop between the two layers at the side seam. Sew all the way around the bottom opening with a 1 cm seam, leaving a 5 cm gap unsewn. Pull the mitt through the gap to turn everything right side out.

Step 13: Tuck the gap edges inward, press the entire mitt flat, and topstitch all the way around the bottom opening 2 mm from the edge to close the gap and give a clean finish.

Bonus Kitchen Items

The following items are so simple they don't need a pattern page — just a few measurements and you're ready to go.

Napkins

Cut a square that is 28 cm × 28 cm. Sew a double rolled hem on all four sides — fold each edge 0.5 cm inward and press, then fold again 1 cm and press, then sew. Feel free to adjust the size — smaller cocktail napkins are around 20 cm × 20 cm and larger dinner napkins can go up to 40 cm × 40 cm.

Kitchen Towel

Cut a rectangle that is 42 cm × 62 cm. Sew a double rolled hem on all four sides the same way as the napkins, or attach bias tape along all edges for a more decorative finish.

Coasters

- Circle coasters: cut a circle 16 cm in diameter
- Square coasters: cut a square 20 cm × 20 cm

For both shapes, follow the same quilting method used for the oven mitts on page 27 — layer your fabric with batting, quilt across the surface, then cut your shape. Finish the raw edges with bias tape or binding as shown on page 11. Make sets of 4 or 6 for a complete table setting.

Placemats

Choose your desired size — a standard placemat is about 30 cm × 45 cm. Follow the exact same method as the coasters above — quilt your fabric sandwich first, then cut to size and finish the edges with bias tape or binding.

Reusable Bowl Covers

These are a great eco-friendly alternative to plastic wrap and make a wonderful handmade gift.

Step 1: Place your bowl upside down on your fabric and trace around it with chalk. Remove the bowl and draw a second circle 5 cm outside your first line — this outer line is your cutting line. Cut along the outer circle.

Step 2: Lay your elastic on the wrong side of the fabric, about 1.5 cm from the outer edge, positioning it all the way around the circle. Pin it in place.

Step 3: Fold the edge of the fabric over the elastic toward the wrong side and pin it down, encasing the elastic completely inside the fold. Sew close to the inner fold all the way around, stretching the elastic gently as you sew to keep it taut. When you reach the starting point, overlap your stitches by 1 cm to secure. Tie the elastic ends together firmly inside the casing and trim any excess.

Tip: Make several sizes by tracing different bowls. These also work as covers for cups, jars, and containers.

Business Ideas

You have now completed Chapter 1 — Kitchen Accessories. Every project in this chapter has real selling potential. Here are some ideas to turn your sewing into income:

Personalized and Monogrammed Kitchen Sets

Create matching sets of aprons, chef hats, oven mitts, kitchen towels, pot holders, and coasters in coordinating fabrics. Add embroidered names, initials, or fun sayings for a personalized touch. These make exceptional gifts for weddings, housewarmings, Mother's Day, and family occasions. Consider offering sets tailored to families — matching aprons for parents and children are especially popular.

Victorian Aprons

There is a growing market for cottagecore and vintage-style clothing. Victorian aprons appeal to women who love that aesthetic — market them to this audience on platforms like Etsy, Instagram, and Pinterest where visual style sells.

Customizable Restaurant Uniforms

Approach local restaurants, cafés, and bakeries to offer personalized uniform aprons with their logo or name embroidered or printed on them. This is a reliable B2B income stream that can generate repeat orders.

Marketing Strategies

- Share your creations with family, friends, and neighbors first — word of mouth is the most powerful and free marketing tool available.
- Set up a shop on Etsy or Facebook Marketplace to reach buyers beyond your local area.
- Create dedicated social media pages on Instagram and TikTok to showcase your work — short videos of the making process perform particularly well and attract both buyers and followers.
- Partner with local kitchenware shops, boutiques, or food markets to display and sell your items.

Photography Matters

High-quality photos make a significant difference when selling handmade items online. Natural light, clean backgrounds, and styled flat lays all make your products look more professional and appealing. Invest time in good photography — it directly affects how many sales you make.

Chapter 2
Hair and Beauty

Scrunchies

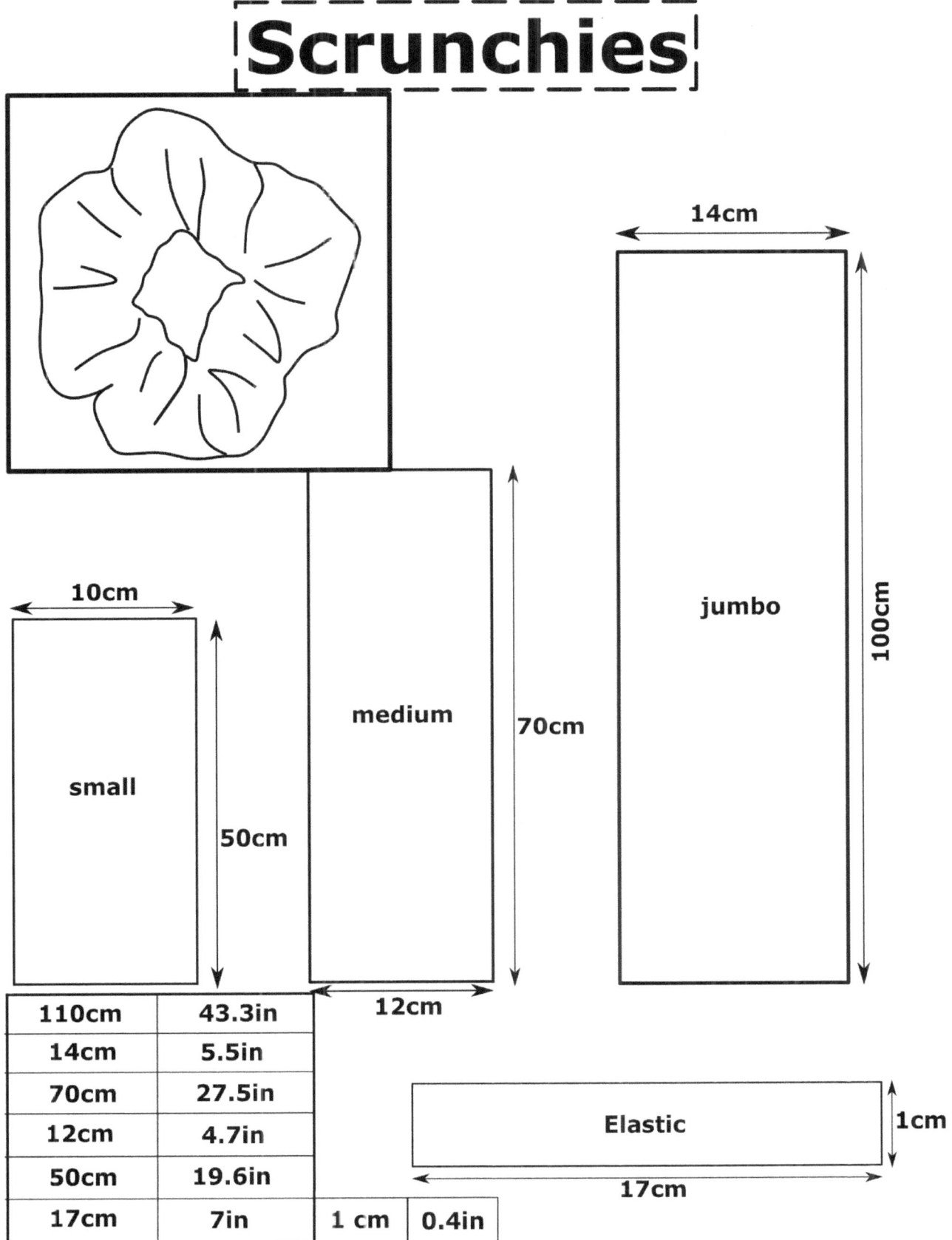

110cm	43.3in
14cm	5.5in
70cm	27.5in
12cm	4.7in
50cm	19.6in
17cm	7in
1 cm	0.4in

Scrunchies

One of the most popular and easiest sewing projects. You can make three sizes — jumbo, medium, and small — all using the same method. Choose satin, velvet, or any fabric you like.

Sizes:
- Jumbo: 110 cm × 14 cm fabric / 17 cm × 1 cm elastic
- Medium: 70 cm × 12 cm fabric / 17 cm × 1 cm elastic
- Small: 50 cm × 10 cm fabric / 17 cm × 1 cm elastic

Materials Needed:
- Fabric of your choice (satin recommended)
- Elastic
- Chalk
- Ruler
- Pins
- Scissors

Instructions:

Step 1: Cut your fabric rectangle according to the size you want to make, using the measurements above.

Step 2: Fold your rectangle in half lengthwise with the right sides of the fabric facing each other. Press well. Fold each long raw edge inward by 1 cm toward the center and press again — this hides the raw edges inside.

Step 3: Unfold the rectangle and lay it flat. Bring the two short ends together with right sides facing each other and sew them together with a 1 cm seam, forming a loop. Press the seam flat.

Step 4: Refold the rectangle lengthwise along your original press lines, right sides together, so the raw edges line up. Sew along the long open edge with a 1 cm seam, leaving a 2 cm gap unsewn — this gap is where you will insert the elastic.

Step 5: Turn the tube right side out through the 2 cm gap. Press well.

Step 6: Attach a safety pin to one end of your elastic. Insert it into the tube through the gap and push it all the way around until both ends of the elastic come out of the same gap. Overlap the two ends of the elastic by about 1 cm and sew them together securely.

Step 7: Push the elastic back into the tube and distribute the fabric gathers evenly around it. Topstitch the 2 cm gap closed, or close it neatly with an invisible hand stitch.

Double Layer Scrunchie

A fuller, more luxurious scrunchie made with two layers of fabric — a satin base and a sheer layer of organza, lace, or tulle on top.

Materials Needed:
- Satin fabric
- Organza, lace, or tulle
- Elastic
- Chalk
- Ruler
- Pins
- Scissors

Instructions:

Step 1: Cut one organza rectangle measuring 70 cm × 14.5 cm. This will be your outer sheer layer.

Step 2: Cut one satin fabric rectangle measuring 70 cm × 12 cm. This will be your inner layer.

Step 3: Fold your satin rectangle in half lengthwise with right sides together and press. Do the same with your organza rectangle.

Step 4: Open both rectangles flat. Lay the organza rectangle on top of the satin rectangle, unfolded, aligning them along one long edge — the organza will be wider and will extend slightly beyond the satin on both sides.

Step 5: Fold both layers together lengthwise — as if you are folding them as one piece — with right sides facing each other. Sew along the long open edge with a 1 cm seam. Turn right side out and press. You now have a double-layered tube with the organza visible on the outside.

Step 6: Follow Steps 3 through 7 from the basic scrunchie instructions on the previous page — sew the short ends into a loop, insert the elastic, overlap the ends, sew, and close the gap.

Tip: Adjust the proportions of organza to create more or less volume — a wider organza strip will create a fluffier, more dramatic scrunchie.

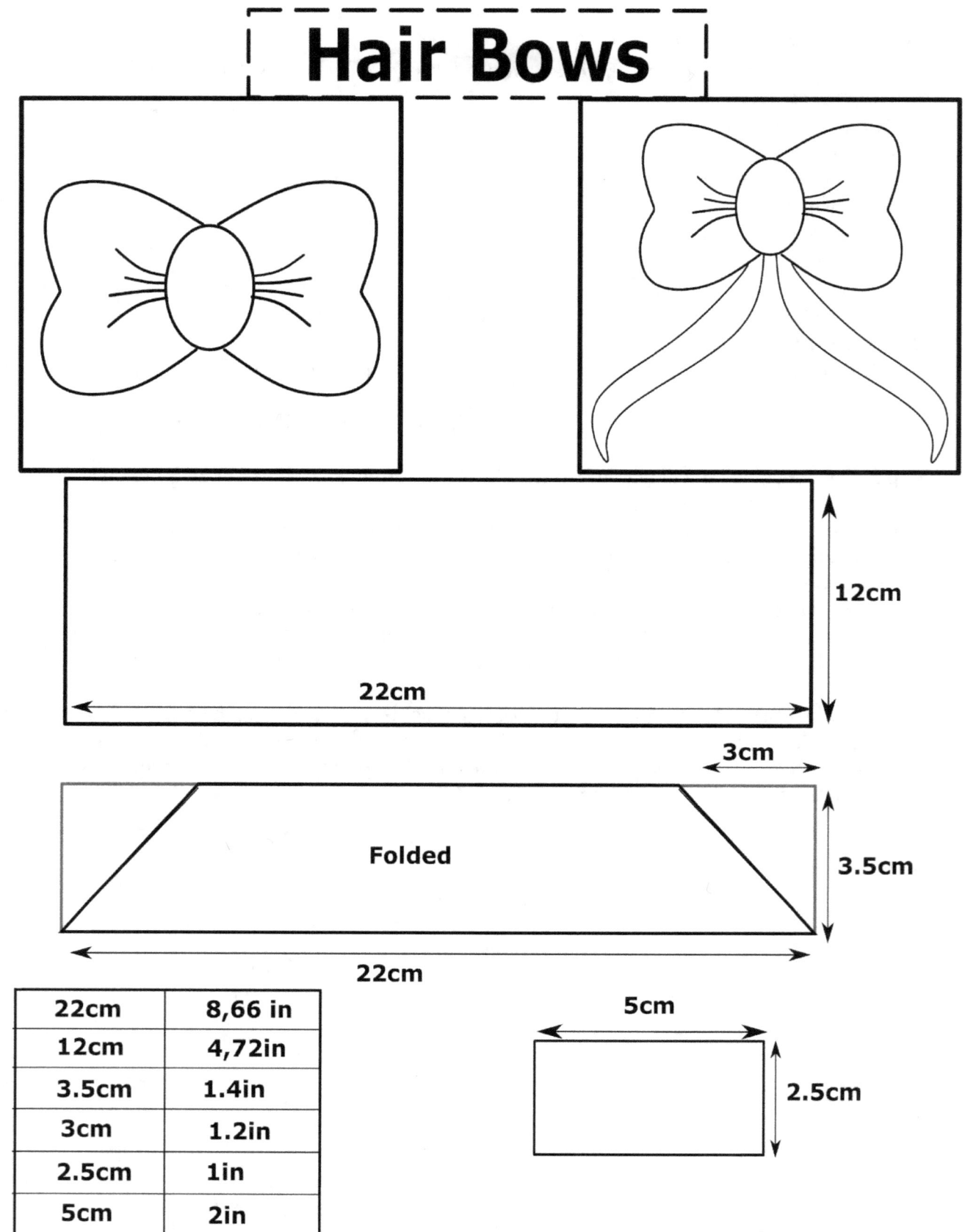

Hair Bows

Two bow styles using the same base method — a classic flat bow and a bow with elegant tails. Both can be made in three sizes.

Materials Needed:
- Fabric of your choice
- Needle and thread
- Chalk
- Ruler
- Pins
- Scissors
- Hair clip or elastic band

Classic Hair Bow

Step 1: Using the size table below, cut your bow body rectangle and your small center knot strip.

Step 2: Fold the bow body rectangle in half lengthwise with right sides facing each other. Sew along the long open edge with a 1 cm seam to create a tube. Turn it right side out using a loop turner or pencil and press flat so the seam runs along the center back.

Step 3: Bring both short raw ends toward the center back of the tube, overlapping them by about 1 cm so the raw edges are hidden inside. Pin in place — you should now have a flat oval loop.

Step 4: Thread your needle and sew a running stitch across the exact center of the oval, going through all layers. Pull the thread firmly to gather the center and create the bow shape. Wrap the thread around the gathered center several times and tie a secure knot to hold the gathers in place.

Step 5: Take your center knot strip. Fold both long edges inward by 0.5 cm toward the wrong side and press. Wrap this strip tightly around the gathered center of your bow, covering the thread. Fold the raw end under and hand stitch it securely at the back.

Step 6: Sew or glue a hair clip to the back of the bow. Alternatively, attach an elastic band to the back center for a hair tie bow.

Size	Bow Body	Center Knot
Jumbo	32 cm × 16 cm	3 cm × 5 cm
Medium	22 cm × 12 cm	2.5 cm × 5 cm
Small	17 cm × 8 cm	2.5 cm × 5 cm

Note: You can make the center knot strip wider if you prefer a chunkier knot.

Hair Bow with Tails

The same classic bow with two elegant ribbon tails hanging down — perfect for a more romantic or vintage look.

Follow the exact same steps as the Classic Hair Bow above, with one addition: before wrapping your center knot strip in Step 5, take your tails piece and fold it in half so both short ends meet in the middle. Pinch it in the center to create a small V shape. Place the tails behind your gathered bow center, with the folded middle tucked under the bow. Use the same thread you used to gather the bow to wrap around and secure the tails at the same time. Then attach your center knot strip over everything to finish.

Size	Bow Body	Center Knot	Tails
Jumbo	32 cm × 16 cm	3 cm × 5 cm	27 cm × 8 cm
Medium	22 cm × 12 cm	2.5 cm × 5 cm	22 cm × 7 cm
Small	17 cm × 8 cm	2.5 cm × 5 cm	17 cm × 6 cm

Note: Tails can be longer or shorter — adjust freely to your preference.

Heatless Hair Curler

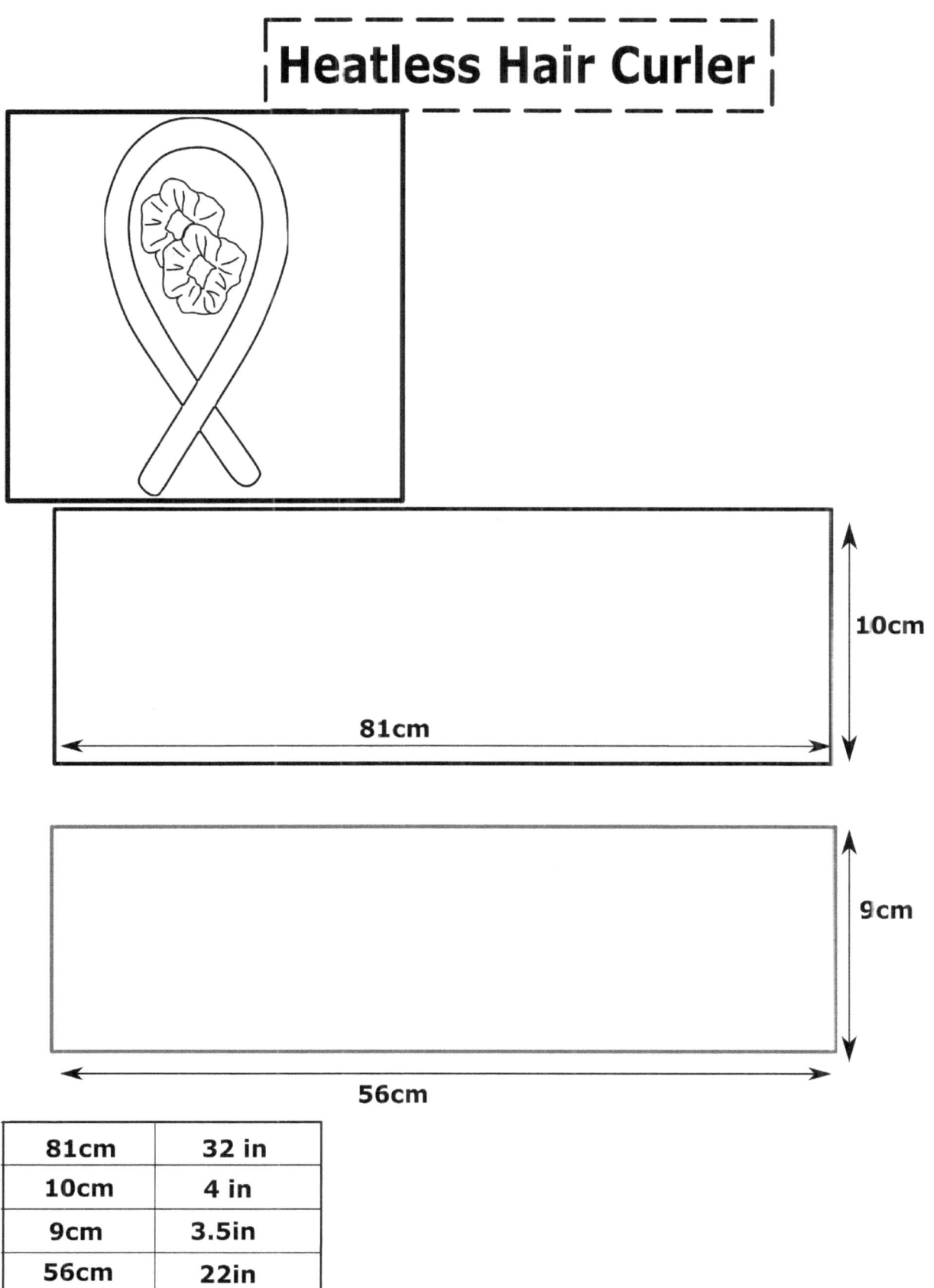

81cm	32 in
10cm	4 in
9cm	3.5in
56cm	22in

Heatless Hair Curler

A soft, padded rod you wrap your hair around overnight to create heatless curls. Comes with two small scrunchies to hold the hair in place.

Materials Needed:
- Satin or silk fabric
- Elastic
- Polyfill stuffing
- Chalk
- Ruler
- Pins
- Scissors

Instructions:

The Curler Rod:

Step 1: Cut a rectangle that is 81 cm × 10 cm from your satin or silk fabric. Fold it in half lengthwise with right sides facing each other and sew along the long open edge with a 1 cm seam, creating a long tube.

Step 2: Turn the tube right side out using a loop turner or safety pin. Press flat.

Step 3: Fold the raw edges of one short end inward by 1 cm and topstitch it closed.

Step 4: Through the remaining open short end, stuff the tube firmly with Polyfill until it is plump and holds its shape well.

Step 5: Fold the raw edges of the remaining open end inward by 1 cm and topstitch it closed. Your curler rod is ready.

The Two Scrunchies:

Cut two rectangles, each 56 cm × 9 cm. Make each one into a scrunchie using either the basic or double layer method from the previous pages. These scrunchies are used to wrap around the rod and hold your hair in place while curling.

How to use: Divide your hair into two sections. Place the curler rod at the top of your head. Wrap one section of hair around one half of the rod all the way down. Secure the end with one of the scrunchies. Repeat on the other side. Sleep with it in place and remove in the morning for soft curls.

Twisted Headband

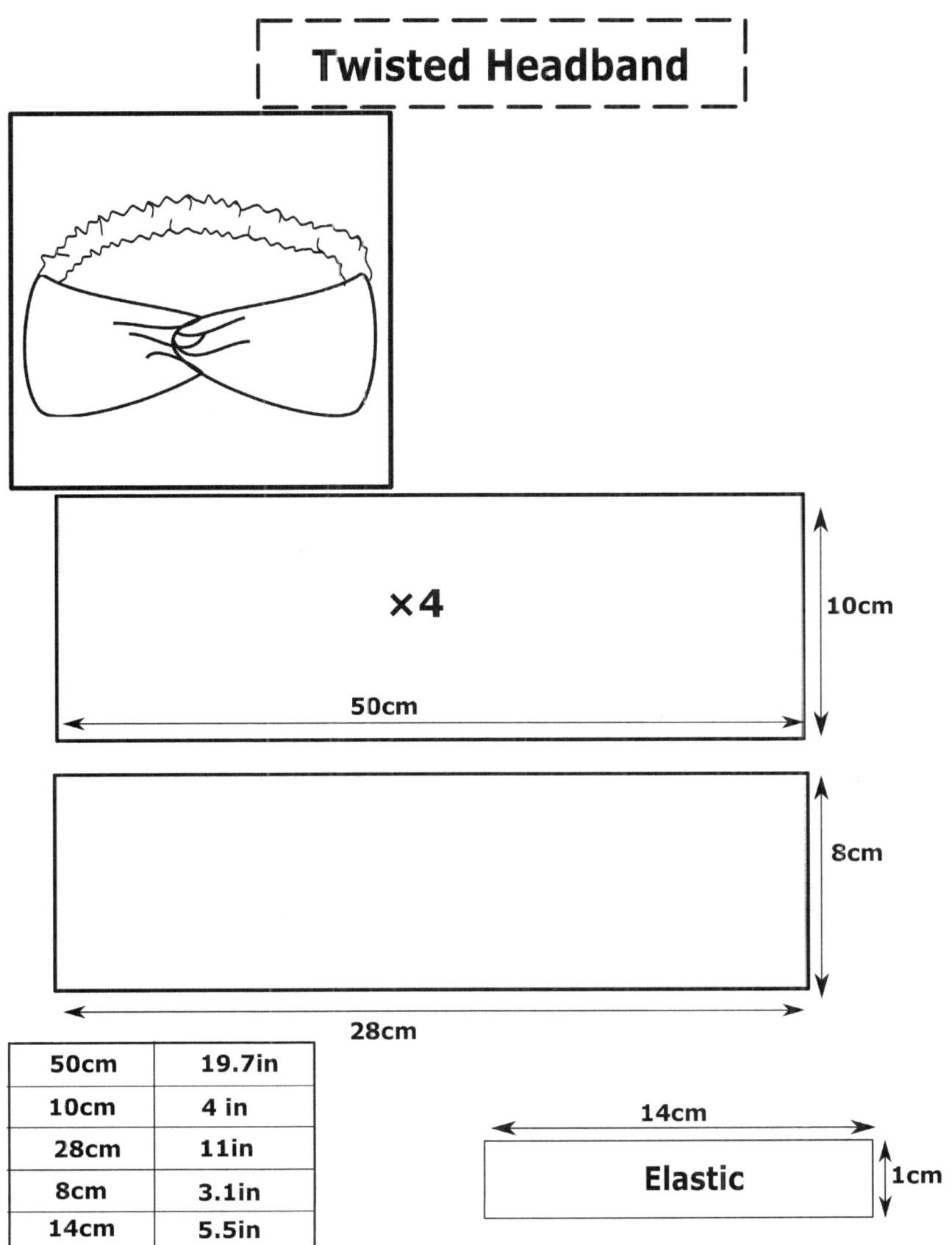

50cm	19.7in
10cm	4 in
28cm	11in
8cm	3.1in
14cm	5.5in

Twisted Headband

A stylish knotted headband with an elastic back for a comfortable fit. The twist in the front is what gives it its signature look.

Materials Needed:
- Satin or any fabric of your choice
- Elastic (1 cm wide)
- Chalk
- Ruler
- Pins
- Scissors

Instructions:

Step 1: Cut 4 rectangles, each 50 cm × 10 cm. These will form the two front panels of the headband.

Step 2: Take two rectangles and place them on top of each other with right sides facing. Sew along both long edges with a 1 cm seam. Repeat with the remaining two rectangles — you now have two sewn tubes.

Step 3: Cut one rectangle that is 28 cm × 8 cm. Fold it in half lengthwise with right sides facing and sew along the long edge. This will be the back elastic casing.

Step 4: Turn all three tubes right side out and press flat.

Step 5: Attach a safety pin to your elastic and insert it into the 28 cm casing tube. Sew the elastic securely to both ends of the casing tube. The elastic should gather the casing slightly — this is the stretchy back part of the headband.

Step 6: Take one of the long front panels. Fold one end over by about 1 cm so the raw edge is hidden, then press. Align this folded end with one raw end of the elastic casing. Wrap the folded panel end around the elastic casing end, encasing it completely, and sew it in place securely. This joins the front panel to the back elastic.

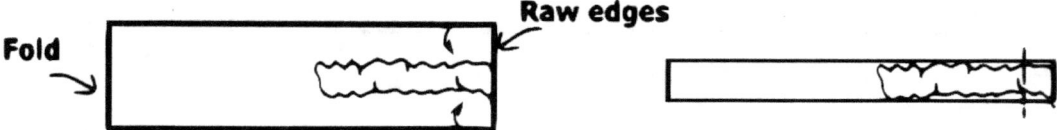

Step 7: Take the second long front panel and pass it through the loop of the first panel — pulling it through completely so the two panels form a knot or twist in the center. This creates the signature twisted look.

Step 8: Take the free end of the second panel, fold the raw edge inward by 1 cm and press. Attach it to the other end of the elastic casing the same way you did in Step 6, encasing the raw end neatly. Sew securely. Flip the headband to the right side for the finished look.

Hair Towel Wrap

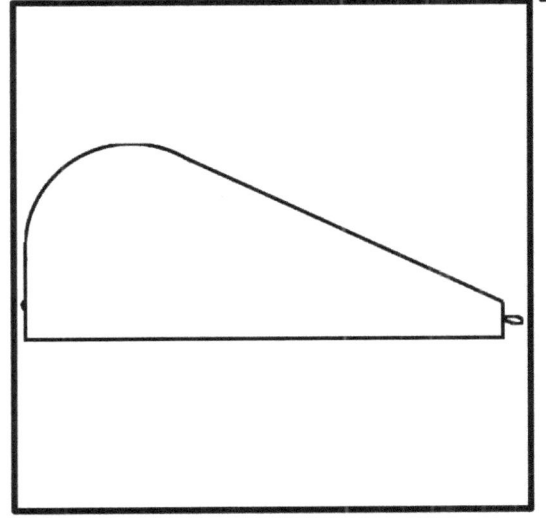

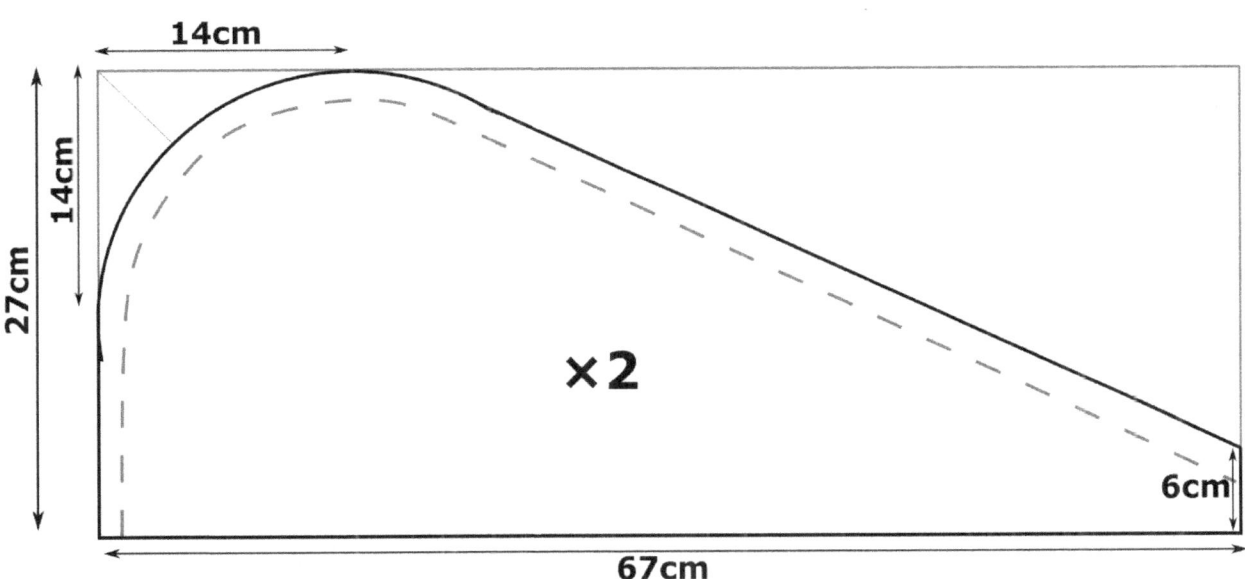

67cm	26.4in
27cm	10.6in
14cm	5.5in
6cm	2.4in
10cm	4in

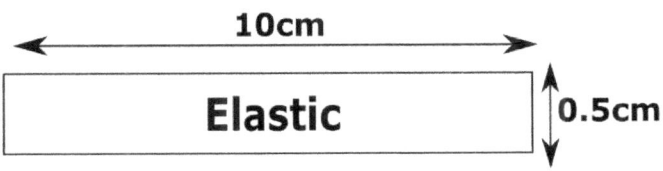

Hair Towel Wrap

A quick-drying microfiber hair wrap that stays on your head without slipping — far more practical than a regular towel. The button and elastic loop keep it secure.

Materials Needed:
- Microfiber fabric
- Elastic (0.5 cm wide)
- Button
- Bias tape (150 cm)
- Chalk
- Ruler
- Pins
- Scissors

Instructions:

Step 1: Using the diagram on the facing page as your guide, draft your pattern on paper. The shape starts as a large rectangle (67 cm × 27 cm) with one corner rounded into a smooth curve — start the curve 14 cm from the top left corner and bring it down 14 cm along the left side. The right end tapers to a point at 6 cm from the bottom. Transfer this shape onto your fabric and cut 2 identical pieces.

Step 2: You will need 150 cm of bias tape. If you don't have it, cut a strip of fabric that is 150 cm × 4 cm on the bias direction and make your own as shown on page 11.

Step 3: Place your two main pieces on top of each other with right sides together. Fold your 10 cm elastic piece in half to form a small loop. Tuck the loop between the two fabric layers at the pointed end of the towel, with the raw ends of the loop aligned with the raw edges of the fabric. Pin everything in place. Sew along the curved top edge only — the dashed lines shown in the diagram — securing the elastic loop inside the seam as you pass over it.

Step 4: Attach your bias tape all the way around the remaining raw edges, enclosing them neatly. Topstitch to secure.

Step 5: Turn the towel to the right side. On the opposite end from the elastic loop, sew a button about 3 cm from the bottom straight edge. Make sure the button is on the outside surface — the side opposite to where you sewed the elastic loop.

To use: Flip your hair forward, place the pointed end at the nape of your neck, flip the towel up over your head, and secure the elastic loop over the button at the front.

Satin hair bonnet

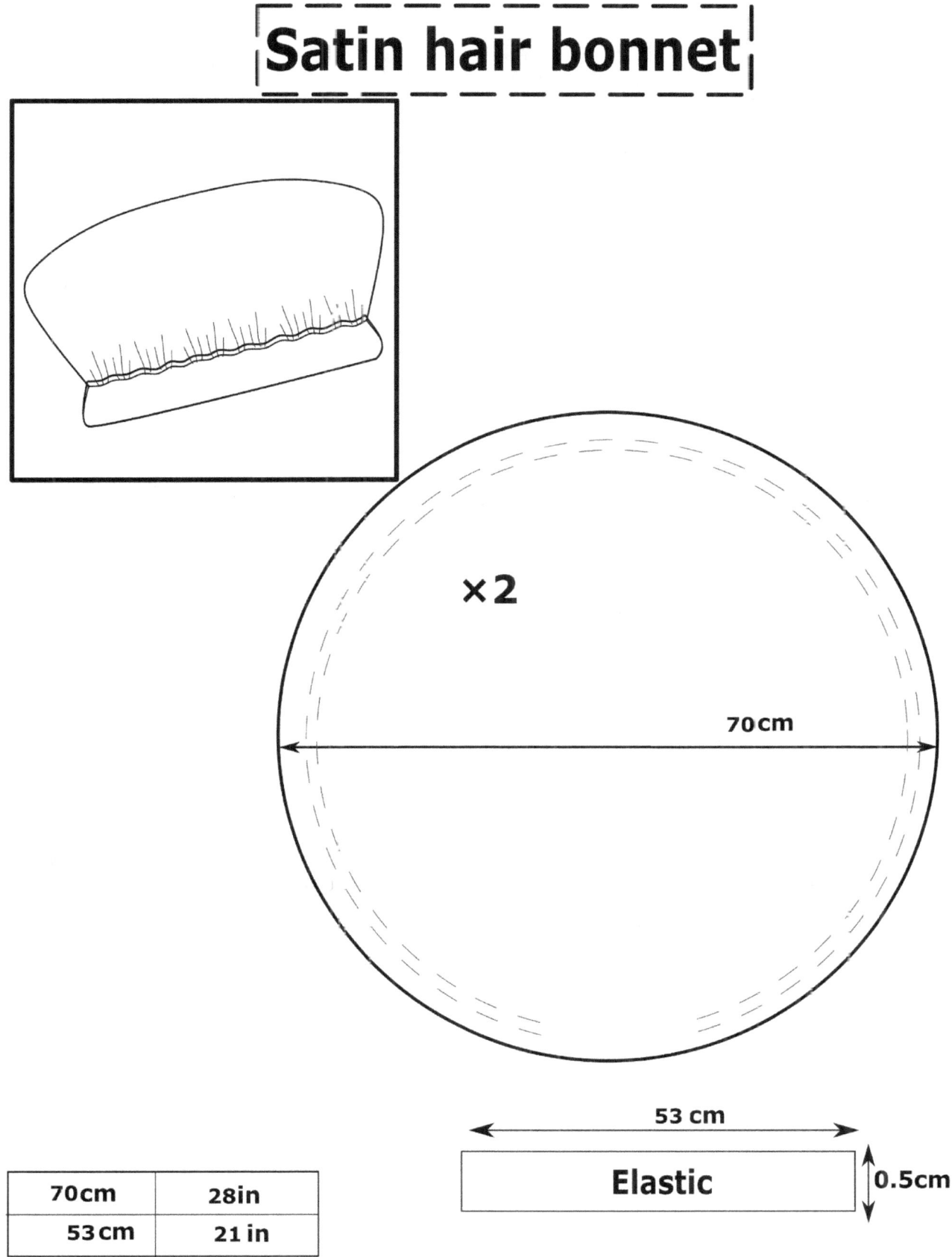

70 cm	28 in
53 cm	21 in

Satin Hair Bonnet

A reversible satin sleep bonnet to protect your hair while you sleep. Made from two circles of satin with an elastic casing sewn in.

Materials Needed:
- Satin fabric (two colors for a reversible bonnet, or one color)
- Elastic (0.5 cm wide)
- Chalk
- Ruler
- Scissors
- Pins

Instructions:

Step 1: Cut 2 circles from your satin fabric, each 70 cm in diameter — one from each color if making a reversible bonnet.

Step 2: Place both circles on top of each other with right sides facing. Sew all the way around the outer edge with a 1 cm seam, leaving a 5 cm gap unsewn. Backstitch at the start and end of your stitching.

Step 3: Clip small notches all around the curved edge close to the stitching — this helps the seam lie flat. Turn the bonnet right side out through the 5 cm gap and press well so the edges are smooth and flat.

Step 4: Now you will sew the elastic casing. Measure 3 cm in from the outer edge of the bonnet and draw a circle all the way around — this is your first casing stitch line. Sew along this line, but leave a small 2 cm gap in the stitching so you can insert the elastic later.

Step 5: Measure 0.7 cm inward from your first stitched line and draw another circle parallel to it. Sew along this second line, again leaving a small 2 cm gap. The channel between these two stitch lines is your elastic casing.

Step 6: Attach a safety pin to your elastic (53 cm long). Insert it into the casing through one of the gaps and push it all the way around until both ends come out of the same gap. Overlap the ends of the elastic by 1 cm and sew them together. Pull the joined elastic back into the casing.

Step 7: Topstitch the two casing gaps closed.

Step 8: Close the original 5 cm turning gap from Step 2 using an invisible stitch or topstitch.

Note: These are standard measurements. For a personalized fit, measure around your head and use that measurement for the elastic length. The circle diameter can range between 25 cm and 35 cm radius depending on your head size.

Cottagecore bandana

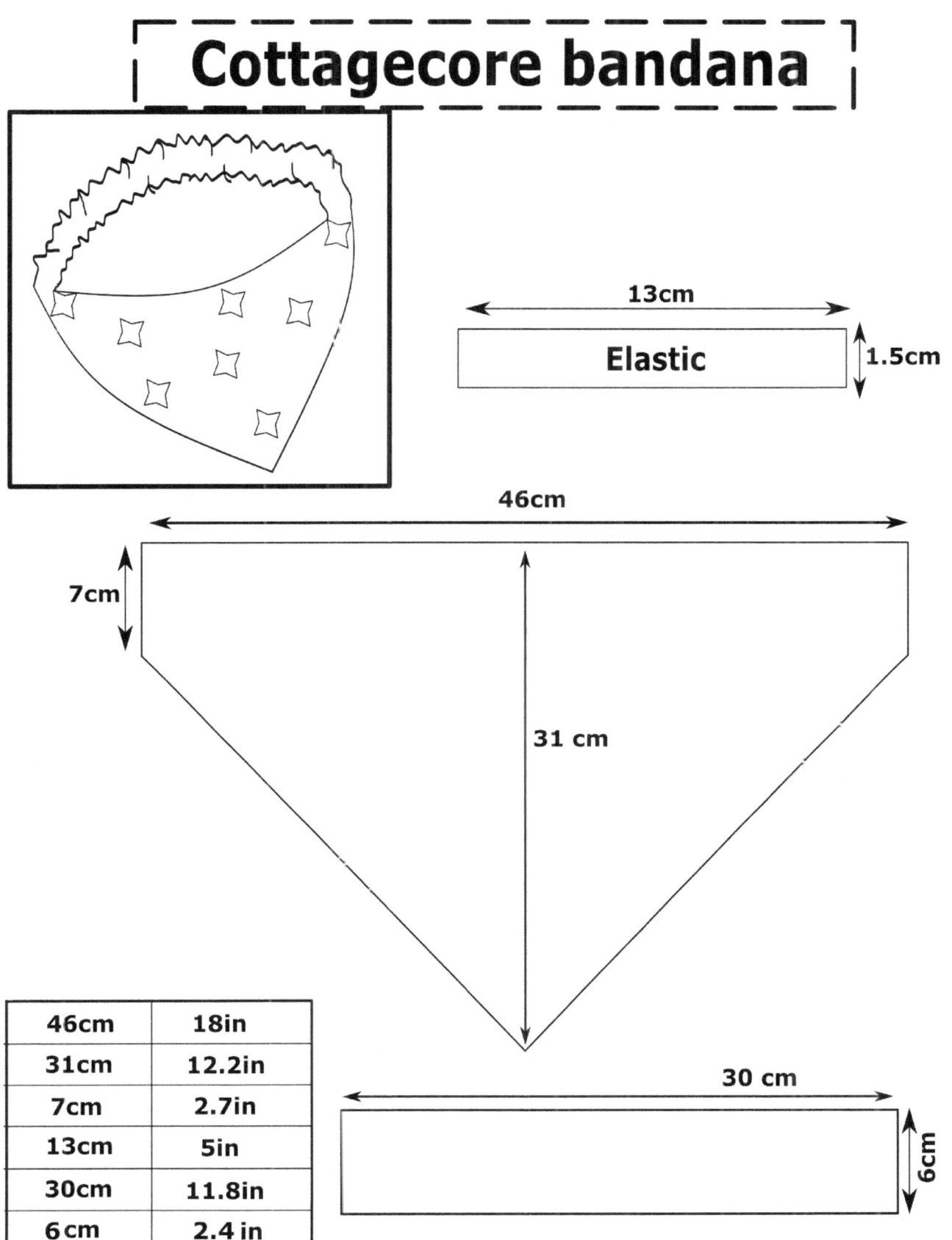

46cm	18in
31cm	12.2in
7cm	2.7in
13cm	5in
30cm	11.8in
6 cm	2.4 in

Cottagecore Bandana

A triangular headscarf with a gathered elastic back — easy to wear and perfect for a vintage or cottagecore aesthetic. Use any patterned fabric for the best look.

Materials Needed:

- Fabric of your choice (patterned recommended)
- Elastic (1.5 cm wide)
- Chalk
- Ruler
- Pins
- Scissors

Instructions:

Step 1: Using the diagram on the facing page as your guide, draft your pattern. The main piece is a large triangle — 46 cm wide at the top and 31 cm tall — with the top edge straight and the two sides tapering to a point at the bottom. The top edge has a 7 cm fold-down area marked with a dashed line. Cut 1 piece from your fabric. Also cut one casing strip that is 30 cm × 6 cm.

Step 2: Take your casing strip and fold it in half lengthwise with right sides together. Sew along the long open edge with a 1 cm seam. Turn it right side out and press flat — this is now a flat tube for your elastic.

Step 3: Insert your elastic (13 cm long) into the casing tube. Sew across both short ends of the casing to secure the elastic inside — the elastic should be gathered inside, making the casing pucker slightly.

Step 4: On the main bandana piece, fold and press the two diagonal side edges inward by 0.5 cm, then fold again by 0.5 cm and press. Sew a small hem along both diagonal edges. Do the same for the bottom pointed tip.

Step 5: Fold the top straight edge of the bandana down by 7 cm toward the wrong side and press. This creates the facing for the back.

Step 6: On each end of the top folded edge, place one end of the gathered elastic casing face down on the right side of the fabric, aligning the raw end of the casing with the raw edge of the bandana. The casing should sit in the center of the fabric width. Fold the fabric over the casing, enclosing it, and sew 1 cm from the raw edge to attach it. Repeat on the other side. When you flip the fabric over, the elastic casing sits at the back of the bandana, creating the gathered hair tie effect.

Note: For the best look, use a patterned fabric with a small floral, gingham, or vintage print.

Sleeping eye mask

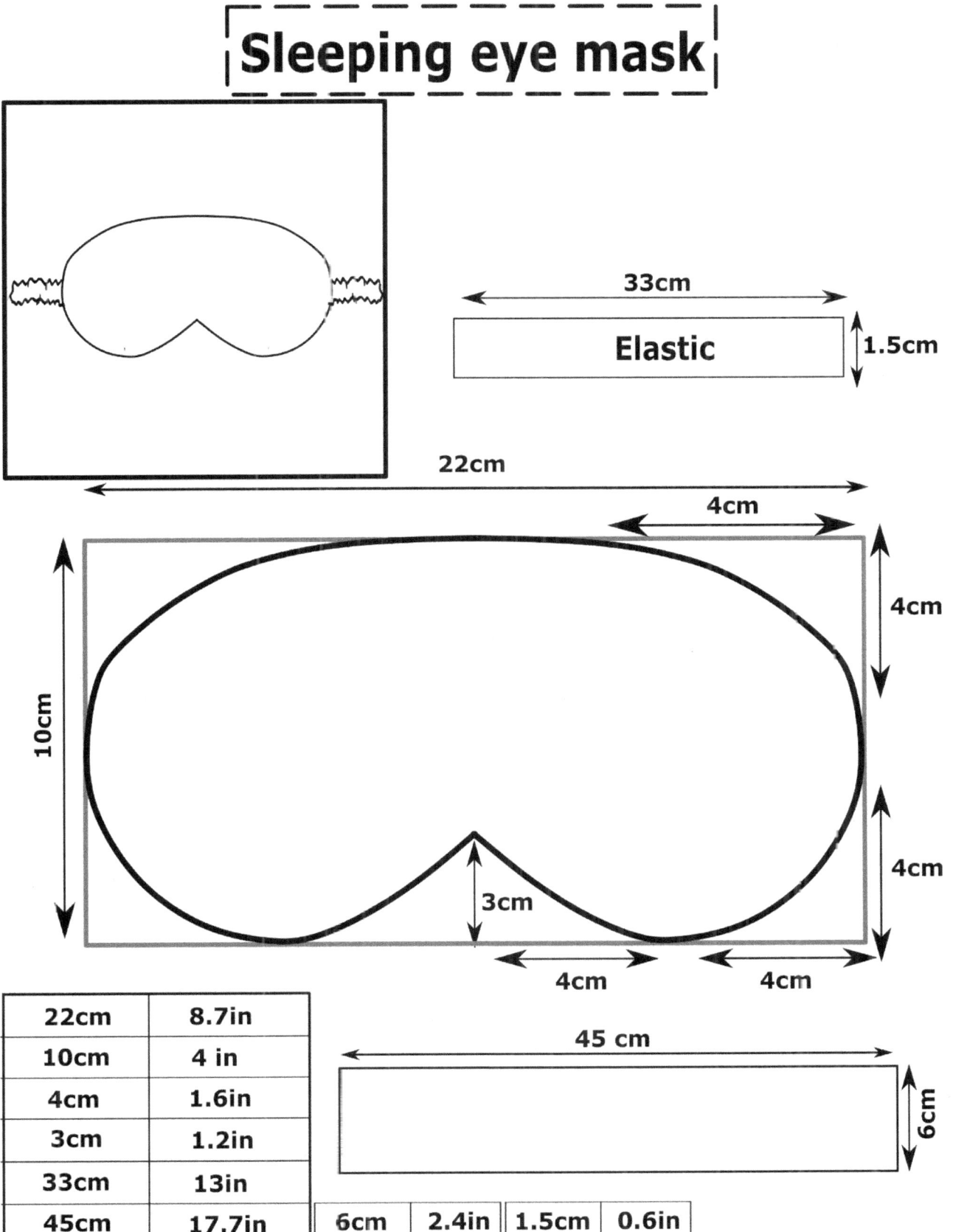

22cm	8.7in
10cm	4 in
4cm	1.6in
3cm	1.2in
33cm	13in
45cm	17.7in

| 6cm | 2.4in | 1.5cm | 0.6in |

Sleeping Eye Mask

A padded sleep mask with a satin outer shell and soft fusible fleece lining for total comfort. The elastic casing at the back keeps it in place while you sleep.

Materials Needed:
- Satin fabric
- Fusible fleece
- Elastic (1.5 cm wide)
- Chalk
- Ruler
- Pins
- Scissors

Instructions:

Step 1: Using the diagram on the facing page as your guide, draft your mask pattern on paper. The shape is an oval 22 cm wide and 10 cm tall, with a gentle V-shaped dip at the bottom center — 3 cm deep, with each side of the V starting 4 cm from the center. Cut 2 pieces from your satin fabric and 1 piece from your fusible fleece.

Step 2: Cut one casing strip that is 45 cm × 6 cm from your satin fabric. Fold it in half lengthwise with right sides together and sew along the long edge with a 1 cm seam. Turn it right side out and press — this is your elastic casing tube.

Step 3: Take one satin mask piece and iron the fusible fleece onto its wrong side. This adds padding and structure to your mask.

Step 4: Lay the fleece-backed mask piece flat with the right side facing up. Cut your elastic to 33 cm. Fold it in half and place the folded midpoint at the center of one side edge of the mask — the raw ends of the elastic should point outward beyond the edge of the mask. Pin the elastic in place. Place the second mask piece on top with its right side facing down — so both right sides are facing each other with the elastic sandwiched between them at the side.

Step 5: Sew all the way around the outer edge of the mask with a 1 cm seam, leaving a 4 cm gap along the top straight edge — this gap is shown by the dashed lines in the diagram. Make sure to catch the elastic ends securely in your seam as you sew past them.

Step 6: Clip small notches all around the curved edges. Turn the mask right side out through the gap, carefully pushing out all curves. Press well.

Step 7: Topstitch all the way around the mask 2 mm from the edge — this closes the gap and gives a polished finish.

Reusable makeup pads

10cm

10cm

10cm

| 10cm | 4 in |

Reusable Makeup Pads

Eco-friendly, washable pads to replace disposable cotton rounds. Make them in any size — 10 cm is standard but you can go larger or smaller.

Materials Needed:
- Microfiber, terry cloth, cotton, or bamboo fabric
- A second layer of fabric (same or contrasting)
- Chalk
- Ruler
- Pins
- Scissors

Note: The top layer can be any soft fabric. The bottom layer, which touches your skin, works best in microfiber or terry cloth. Using two different fabrics gives you two usable sides.

For circle pads:

Step 1: Cut 2 circles per pad, each 10 cm in diameter. Place them on top of each other with right sides facing and sew all the way around the edge with a 1 cm seam, leaving a 2 cm gap unsewn.

Step 2: Clip small notches around the curved edge. Turn the pad right side out through the gap, push the edges out smoothly, and press flat.

Step 3: Topstitch all the way around the pad 2 mm from the edge, closing the gap as you go.

For square pads: Follow the exact same three steps above using 10 cm × 10 cm squares instead of circles. No notching needed for squares — just clip the four corners diagonally before turning.

Tip: Make a set of 7–10 pads so you always have clean ones ready while others are in the wash. Store them in a small drawstring bag.

Exfoliating Body Glove

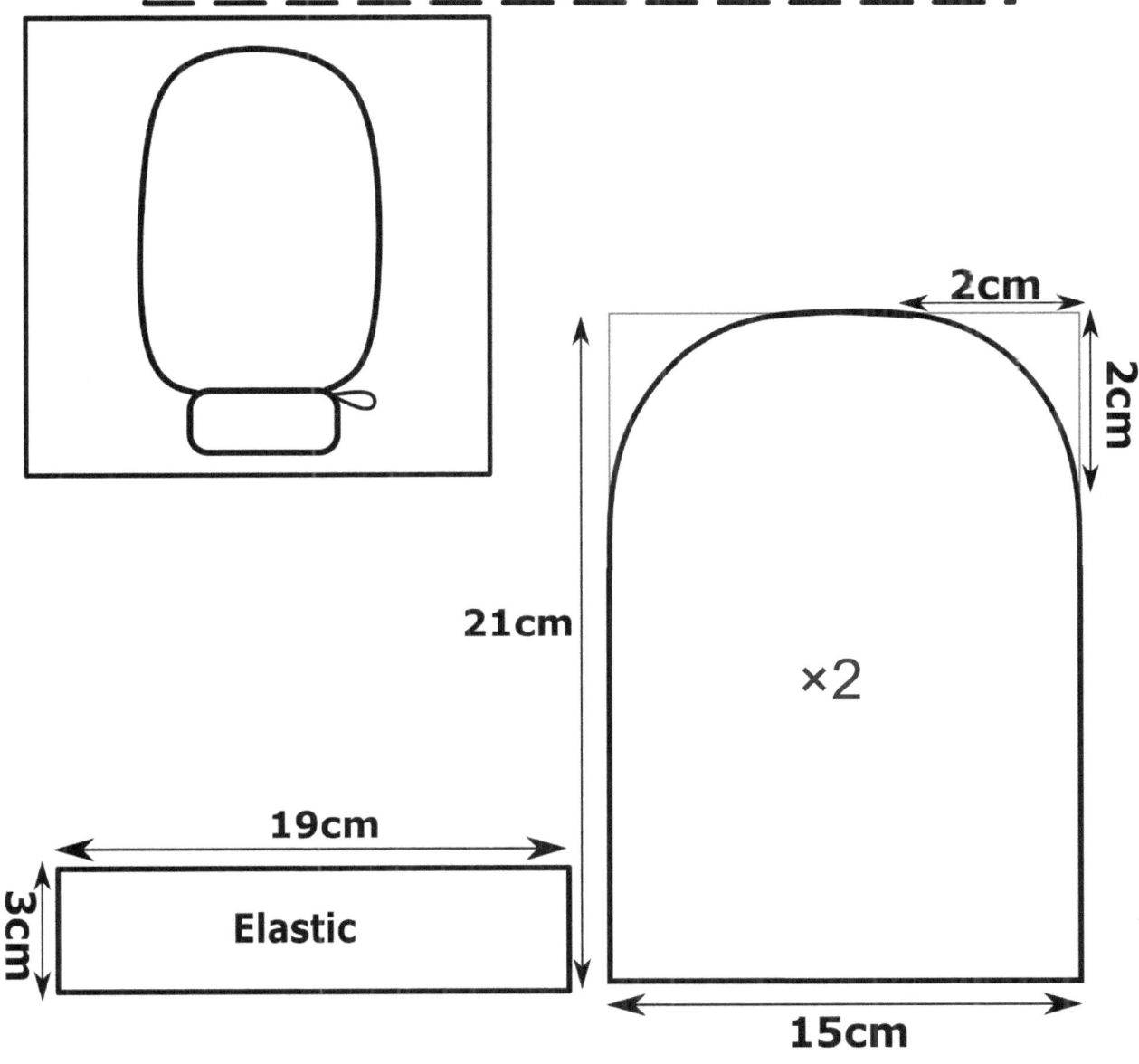

21cm	8.3in
15cm	6in
19cm	7.5in
2cm	0.8in
3cm	1.2in

Exfoliating Body Glove

Also known as an Italy towel or Korean spa mitt — a bath glove used to exfoliate the skin. The key is using the right fabric: textured viscose rayon or viscose linen, which is the rough-textured fabric used in Korean spas. Without this specific fabric the glove will not exfoliate.

Materials Needed:
- Viscose rayon or viscose linen fabric (textured)
- Elastic (3 cm wide, 19 cm long)
- Chalk
- Ruler
- Pins
- Scissors

Instructions:

Step 1: Using the diagram on the facing page as your guide, cut 2 pieces of fabric that are 15 cm wide and 21 cm tall, with the top two corners rounded into a smooth curve — the curve starts 2 cm from each top corner on both the top and side edges.

Step 2: Place the two pieces on top of each other with right sides facing. Sew around all edges with a 1 cm seam, leaving the entire bottom straight edge open.

Step 3: Take your elastic piece. Overlap its two short ends by 1 cm and sew them together to form a closed loop.

Step 4: Pin the elastic loop to the bottom opening of the glove, aligning the raw edge of the elastic with the raw edge of the fabric opening. Sew all the way around the bottom edge with a 1 cm seam, attaching the elastic loop to the glove. Flip the glove right side out — the elastic will now sit inside, forming the wrist opening.

Note: For a simpler version, cut two rectangles instead of the curved shape and sew them together on three sides, leaving the bottom open.

Business Ideas
Chapter 2 — Hair and Beauty is full of products with strong market potential, especially in the growing natural hair care and sustainable beauty spaces.

Scrunchie and Hair Bow Gift Sets
Create curated sets of scrunchies in various sizes, colors, and fabrics — velvet, satin, floral cotton — and package them as gift sets. Offer the same for hair bows. Add optional personalized embroidery to make them unique. Sets of 3 or 5 in coordinating colors sell particularly well on Etsy and at craft fairs.

Vintage Style Sets
Bundle hair bows with the cottagecore bandana and a Victorian apron from Chapter 1 for a complete vintage-aesthetic gift set. This cross-chapter bundling adds value and targets the cottagecore, prairie, and vintage style communities — a large and active market on social media.

Healthy Hair Care Pack
Many women follow a dedicated hair care routine focused on reducing heat damage. Bundle the heatless hair curler, satin hair bonnet, and microfiber hair towel wrap into a "Hair Protection Pack." This is a high-value, gift-ready set that appeals to women with curly, natural, or color-treated hair.

Affordable Beauty Products
Reusable makeup pads and exfoliating body gloves are eco-friendly alternatives to expensive disposable products. Market them to eco-conscious buyers looking to reduce waste and save money on beauty routines. Package them in small fabric drawstring bags for a polished presentation.

Night Routine Set
Create a complete nighttime routine set including the satin hair curler, satin bonnet, sleeping eye mask, and scrunchies — all in matching fabrics or colors. These make exceptional self-care gifts and perform very well during holidays and on birthdays.

Personalized Gift Boxes
Offer custom gift boxes combining items from this chapter based on customer preferences — asking buyers which colors, fabrics, and sizes they prefer. Personalization builds customer loyalty and often leads to repeat orders.

Marketing Strategies

Start by sharing your products with friends, family, and neighbors to generate your first word-of-mouth sales. Then move on to building a presence on Instagram and TikTok where beauty and hair care content thrives — short videos of you making and using the products perform extremely well and attract both buyers and followers.

Partner with hair salons, beauty stores, and nail studios in your area to display your products — they attract the exact audience you are targeting.

For photography, shoot during the golden hour — the hour after sunrise or before sunset — for the best natural light without professional equipment. Clean, bright photos with simple backgrounds make a huge difference in how professional your products look online.

Post consistently and research the best times to reach your target audience. Run occasional giveaways to grow your following, but do not overdo them — too many giveaways attract people who are only interested in free products and not genuine buyers.

Interact regularly with your followers through polls, questions, and comments. This builds a loyal customer base and helps you understand what products people want most. If your budget allows, invest in sponsored posts to boost visibility and reach new audiences faster.

Chapter 3 Home Decor

Fitted bedsheets

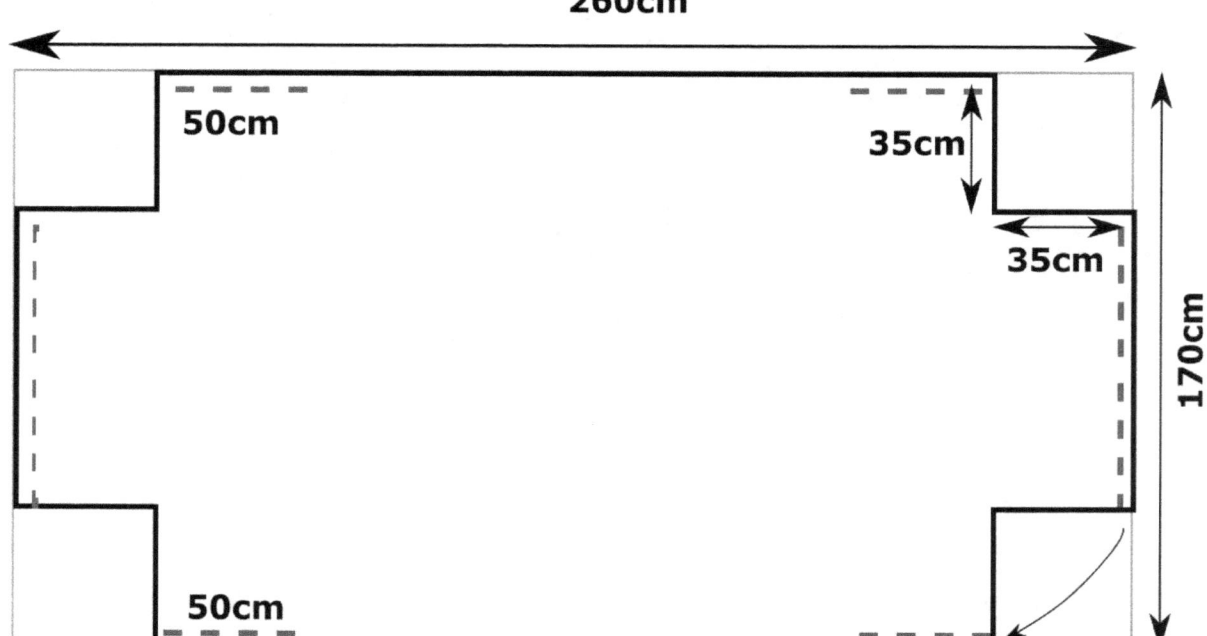

260cm	102in
170cm	67 in
50cm	19.7in
35cm	13.8in

Fitted Bedsheets

A custom fitted sheet that wraps snugly around your mattress. The instructions below use a twin/single mattress (100 cm × 190 cm) as an example, but the fabric calculation formula works for any size.

Materials Needed:
- Fabric (see calculation below for how much you need)
- Elastic
- Chalk
- Ruler
- Pins
- Scissors

How to Calculate Your Fabric:

First measure your mattress — you need three numbers: the width, the length, and the depth (how thick the mattress is).

Then use these two formulas:

Fabric width = mattress width + (depth × 2) + (15 × 2)

Fabric length = mattress length + (depth × 2) + (15 × 2)

The depth × 2 accounts for both sides of the mattress. The 15 cm accounts for the fabric that tucks underneath — you can use 10 cm or 5 cm instead if you prefer less tuck.

Example: For a twin mattress that is 100 cm wide × 190 cm long × 20 cm deep:
- *Fabric width = 100 + (20 × 2) + (15 × 2) = 170 cm*
- *Fabric length = 190 + (20 × 2) + (15 × 2) = 260 cm*

Common Mattress Sizes:

Name	cm	inches
Twin/Single	99 × 191 cm	39 × 75 in
Full/Double	137 × 191 cm	54 × 75 in
Queen	152 × 203 cm	60 × 80 in
King	193 × 203 cm	76 × 80 in

Instructions:

Step 1: Cut your fabric to the calculated width and length. Fold it in half lengthwise, then fold it in half again widthwise — you now have a folded rectangle that is one quarter of the full sheet.

Step 2: On the two corners that have raw edges (not folds), trace and cut a square of 35 cm × 35 cm. These cut-outs are what create the fitted corners. When you unfold the fabric you will see a cross shape with a square notch cut from each corner — just like the diagram on the facing page.

Step 3: On each corner, bring the two raw cut edges together with right sides facing and sew them with a 1 cm seam. This stitching creates the corner pocket that fits over the mattress corners. Do this for all four corners.

Step 4: Mark 50 cm from each corner along the hem edge — these are your elastic zones. Between those marks, sew a plain rolled hem with no elastic.

Step 5: At each marked point, begin the elastic section. Fold the hem over by 0.5 cm and press, then fold again by 1 cm. Place your elastic inside the fold and pin it in place. Sew close to the inner fold, stretching the elastic firmly as you sew through each corner zone — this creates the gathered, fitted look. Trim the elastic at the next mark and continue with the plain hem.

Step 6: Repeat across all four corners. When you are done, each corner should be gathered and the straight sides between them should have a plain flat hem.

Note: You can use elastic all the way around the entire edge instead of just the corners — this gives a tighter, more secure fit and is easier to make. Simply sew a continuous hem with elastic running all the way around.

Envelope Pillowcase

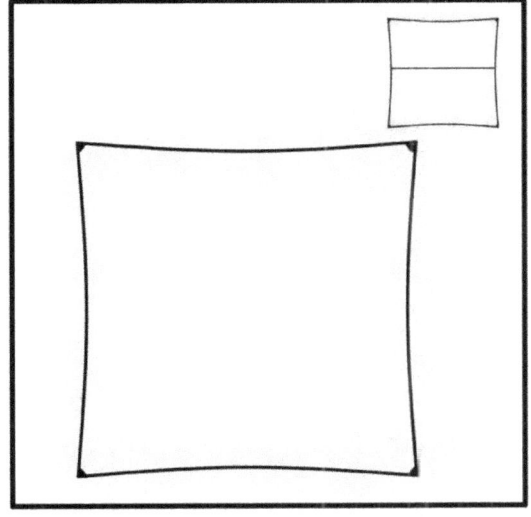

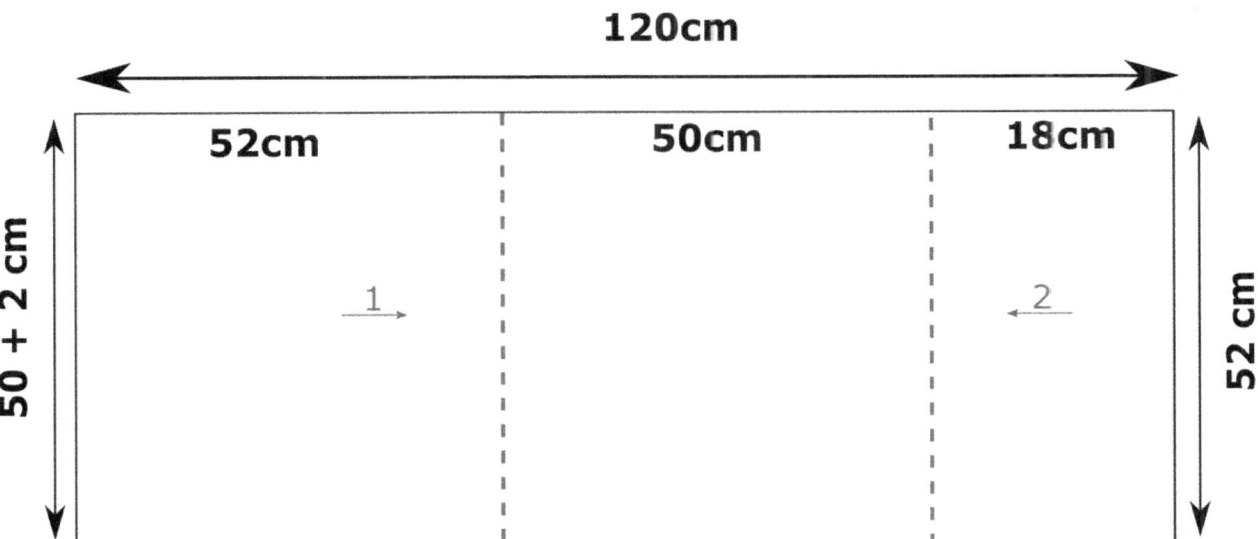

50cm	20in
52cm	21 in
18cm	7in
120cm	47in

Envelope Pillowcase

A pillowcase without buttons or zippers — the back has two overlapping flaps that keep the pillow inside. Clean, simple, and beginner-friendly. This example uses a 50 cm × 50 cm pillow insert.

Materials Needed:
- Fabric of your choice
- Chalk
- Ruler
- Pins
- Scissors

Method 1 — One Piece:

This is the simpler method — just one rectangle of fabric.

Step 1: Cut one rectangle that is 52 cm × 120 cm. The 52 cm is your pillow height plus 2 cm seam allowance. The 120 cm is made up of three sections: 52 cm (front) + 50 cm (back) + 18 cm (overlap flap).

Step 2: On each short end of the rectangle, fold the raw edge inward by 0.5 cm and press. Fold inward again by 1 cm and press. Sew a neat rolled hem on both short ends.

Step 3: Lay your rectangle flat. Looking at the diagram, fold Section 1 (the 52 cm section) over toward the center, right side facing down. Then fold Section 2 (the 18 cm flap) over from the other end, also right side facing down — it will overlap Section 1 in the middle.

Step 4: Pin the top and bottom raw edges and sew all the way along both sides with a 1 cm seam. Clip the four corners diagonally close to the stitching to reduce bulk, then flip the pillowcase right side out through the envelope opening and press.

Method 2 — Three Pieces:

This method gives you more design flexibility — you can use different fabrics for the front and back.

Step 1: Cut one square for the front: 52 cm × 52 cm. Cut two rectangles for the back: each 52 cm × 35.5 cm.

Step 2: On one long edge of each back rectangle, sew a double rolled hem — fold 0.5 cm inward, press, fold again 1 cm, press, and sew. These hemmed edges will be the overlapping opening.

Step 3: Lay the front piece flat with the right side facing up. Place the two back rectangles on top with their right sides facing down, hemmed edges toward the center, overlapping each other in the middle. Pin all four raw edges together.

Step 4: Sew all the way around all four sides with a 1 cm seam. Clip all four corners diagonally. Flip the pillowcase right side out through the envelope opening and press flat.

Sizing Formula:

Method 1: Fabric width = pillow width + 2 cm. Fabric length = (pillow length × 2) + overlap flap (15 cm minimum) + seam allowances.

Method 2: Front = pillow width + 2 cm × pillow length + 2 cm. Each back piece = pillow width + 2 cm × (pillow length ÷ 2) + 15 cm, then cut that rectangle in half along the length.

Zipper Pillowcase: Cut one rectangle of 42 cm × 84 cm. Fold it in half, sew an invisible zipper along the fold line on the wrong side. With right sides together sew the two remaining open sides. Flip right side out through the unzipped opening.

Travel neck pillow

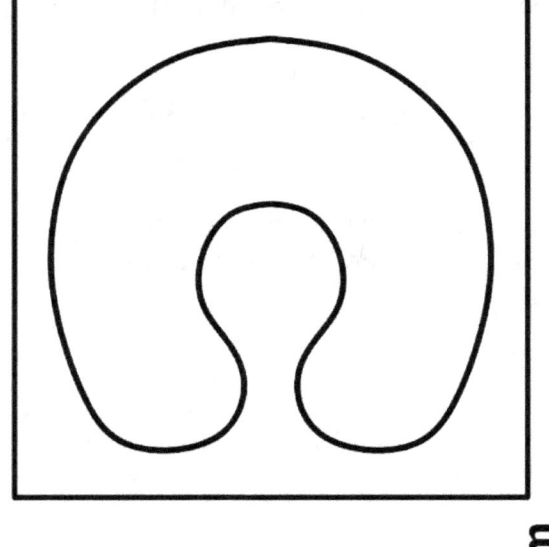

35cm	13.8in
18.5cm	7.3in
13cm	5.1in
14cm	5.5in
11.5cm	4.5in
9cm	3.5in
4.5cm	1.8in
6.5cm	2.4in

Travel Neck Pillow

A U-shaped pillow that supports your neck while traveling or resting. Can be made with or without an invisible zipper for easy washing. Fabrics like cotton, velvet, satin, microfiber, or silk all work well. For filling, use polyester fiberfill, memory foam, or microbeads.

Materials Needed:
- Fabric of your choice
- Polyester fiberfill or other stuffing
- Invisible zipper (optional)
- Chalk
- Ruler
- Pins
- Scissors

Method 1 — Invisible Stitch Closure:

Step 1: Using the diagram on the facing page as your guide, draft your neck pillow pattern on paper and cut 2 pieces from your fabric.

Step 2: Place the two pieces on top of each other with right sides facing. Sew all the way around the outer edge with a 1 cm seam, leaving a 10 cm opening along one of the straight inner edges.

Step 3: Clip small notches all around the curved edges close to the stitching — this is essential for this shape since it has both inner and outer curves. For the inner curve, clip notches. For the outer curve, cut small V-shaped notches. Turn the pillow right side out through the gap and press.

Step 4: Stuff the pillow firmly through the opening with your chosen filling until it feels full and supportive. Close the opening using an invisible stitch.

Method 2 — Invisible Zipper Closure:

Step 1: Cut 2 pieces as before.

Step 2: On one piece, mark where the zipper will start and end along the inner straight edge — leave about 2 cm of clearance from each end. Press the invisible zipper flat with a warm iron to uncurl its teeth.

Step 3: Attach the invisible zipper foot to your sewing machine. Unzip the zipper fully. Place one side of the zipper face down on the right side of one fabric piece, aligning the teeth with your marked line. Sew right alongside the teeth.

Step 4: Repeat with the other side of the zipper on the second fabric piece, making sure both pieces align correctly when the zipper is closed.

Step 5: Zip the zipper closed. With right sides together, sew all the way around the remaining edges with a 1 cm seam. Clip the curves. Unzip the zipper slightly and flip the pillow right side out through the zipper opening. Stuff and zip closed.

Tip: Making two pillows is a great idea — one inner pillow made from cheap muslin, stuffed and stitched closed, and one zippered outer cover in your choice of fabric. This way you can remove and wash the cover without disturbing the stuffing.

Taking Custom Measurements:

To personalize the size, measure around the back of your neck for the inner curve circumference, and measure your shoulder width for the overall outer width of the pillow.

Bean Bag Chair

80cm

×2

40 cm

100 cm

120cm

70cm

100cm	39.4in
120cm	47.2 in
40cm	15.7in
70cm	27.5in
80cm	31.5in

Bean Bag Chair

A cozy floor chair filled with beans, foam, or fiberfill. Made in two parts — an inner bag that holds the filling, and a removable outer cover with a zipper for easy washing.

Materials Needed:
- Outer fabric (soft fabric like velvet, minky, or canvas recommended)
- Inner fabric (old bed sheet, muslin, or canvas)
- Bean bag fillings (EPS beans, polyester fiberfill, or memory foam)
- Zipper (100 cm long)
- Chalk
- Ruler
- Pins
- Scissors

The Inner Bag:
Step 1: Using the diagram on the facing page, cut 4 side panel pieces, 1 large circle (80 cm diameter), and 1 small circle (70 cm diameter) from your inner fabric.
Step 2: Take two side panels and place them together with right sides facing. Sew along one long curved side with a 1 cm seam — refer to the dashed lines in the diagram. Repeat until all 4 panels are sewn together into a cylindrical shape.
Step 3: With right sides together, attach the small circle (70 cm) to the bottom opening of the panel cylinder and sew all the way around with a 1 cm seam.
Step 4: Attach the large circle (80 cm) to the top opening, sewing all the way around but leaving a 15 cm gap unsewn. Flip the inner bag right side out through the gap. Fill it firmly with your chosen filling, then hand stitch the gap closed with an invisible stitch.

The Outer Cover:
Step 1: Cut the same pieces again from your outer fabric — 4 side panels, 1 large circle, 1 small circle.
Step 2: Take two side panels and place them together with wrong sides facing. Sew your 100 cm zipper along both long sides of these two panels — one side of the zipper on each panel — so the zipper runs the full length of one seam. Trim any excess zipper at the ends. Sew the remaining side panel seams together as before.
Step 3: Attach the small circle to the bottom and the large circle to the top, both with right sides together, sewing 1 cm from the edge all the way around.
Step 4: Unzip the zipper slightly to leave an opening. Flip the outer cover right side out through the zipper opening. Insert the filled inner bag, zip the cover closed, and enjoy your bean bag chair.

Note: For the best result, use a soft, durable outer fabric. The zipper allows you to remove the cover for washing without emptying all the filling.

Bolster pillowcase

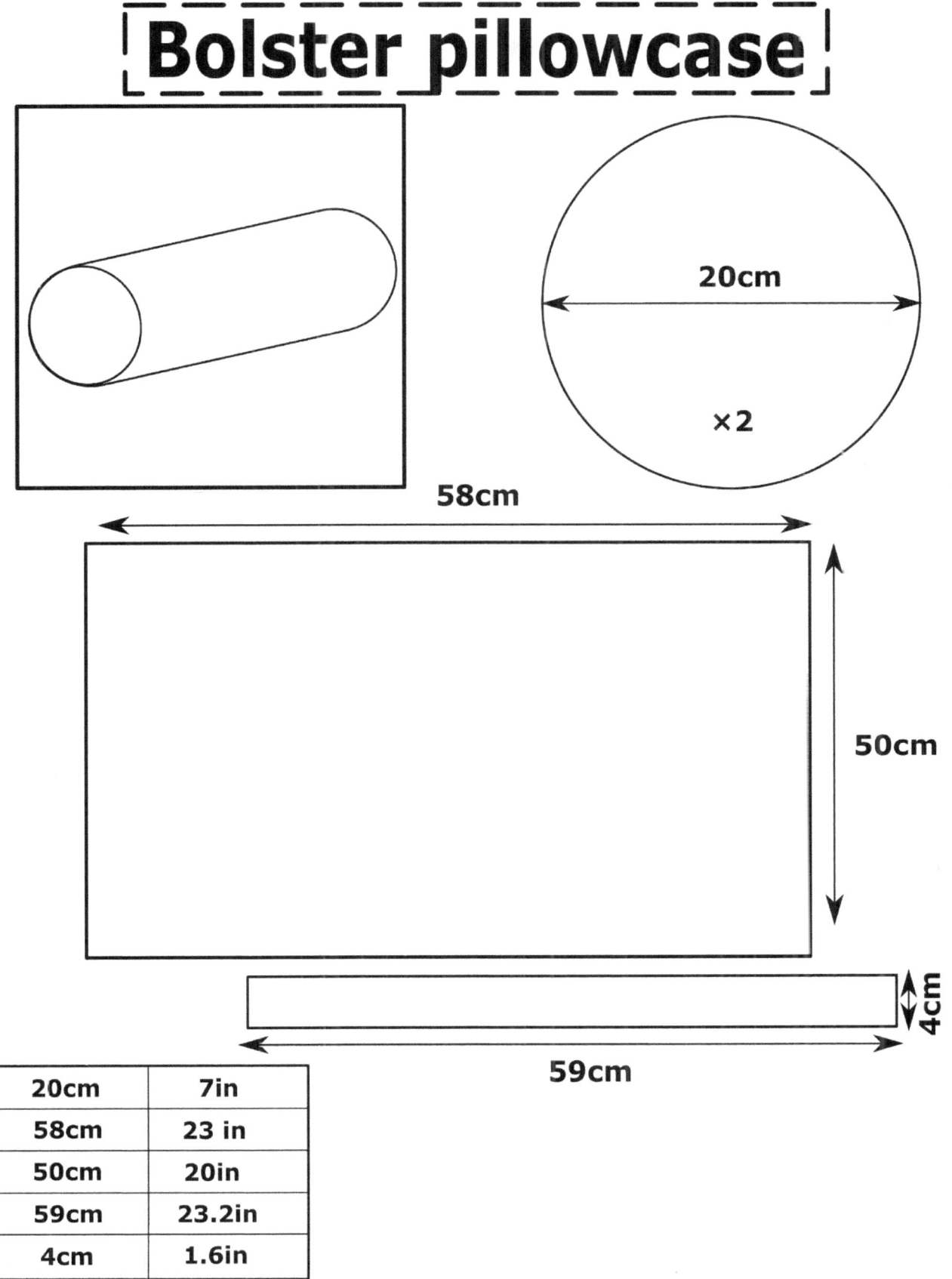

20cm	7in
58cm	23 in
50cm	20in
59cm	23.2in
4cm	1.6in

Bolster Pillowcase

A cylindrical pillowcase with optional piping around the edges for a polished, professional finish. The zipper makes it easy to remove and wash.

Materials Needed:
- Fabric of your choice
- Zipper
- Piping cord (optional)
- Chalk
- Ruler
- Pins
- Scissors

How to Calculate Your Measurements:

Measure your bolster pillow — you need the diameter and the length.

The circumference (how wide to cut the rectangle) = diameter × 3.14, then add 1 cm seam allowance.

Example: For a pillow that is 18 cm in diameter and 48 cm long: Circumference = 18 × 3.14 = 56.5 cm + 1 cm = 57.5 cm (round up to 58 cm)

- Rectangle: 50 cm long × 58 cm wide (length of pillow + 2 cm seam allowance × circumference)
- Two circles: 20 cm in diameter (pillow diameter + 2 cm)
- Two piping strips: 59 cm × 4 cm, cut on the bias

Instructions:

Step 1: Cut your rectangle, two circles, and two piping strips according to your measurements.

Step 2 (Optional — Piping): Fold one piping strip in half lengthwise with wrong sides together and press. Insert your piping cord inside the fold and sew close alongside the cord using a zipper foot — this creates your covered piping. Clip notches along the curved seam allowance so the piping bends easily around the circle. Repeat with the second strip. Skip this step entirely if you want a plain pillowcase.

Step 3: Pin the piping to the right side of each circle, aligning the raw edges of the piping with the raw edge of the circle. Sew all the way around each circle 1 cm from the edge, securing the piping in place.

Step 4: Fold your rectangle in half lengthwise with right sides together. Sew your zipper along the long open edge — for a regular zipper, place it face down on the right side, sew one side, then sew the other side of the zipper to the other fabric edge. For an invisible zipper, press it flat first, then sew each side separately. Stitch across both ends of the zipper to secure them.

Step 5: With right sides together, pin one circle to one opening of the cylinder. Sew all the way around with a 1 cm seam. Unzip the zipper about 10 cm to create an opening, then attach the second circle to the other end the same way. Flip the pillowcase right side out through the unzipped opening. Insert your pillow and zip closed.

How to Sew a Zipper (Beginner Guide):

Step 1: On both fabric pieces, mark where the zipper starts and ends.

Step 2: Place the zipper face down on the right side of one fabric piece, aligning the zipper tape edge with the raw fabric edge. Pin in place.

Step 3: Attach the zipper foot to your machine. Unzip the zipper halfway so you can sew past the pull without stopping. Sew alongside the zipper teeth from top to bottom. When you reach the zipper pull, lower the needle into the fabric, lift the presser foot, slide the pull past the needle, lower the foot again, and continue sewing.

Step 4: Repeat on the other side of the zipper with the second fabric piece.

Step 5: Finish the raw edges beside the zipper with a zigzag stitch or serger to prevent fraying.

For an invisible zipper: press it flat with an iron before sewing to uncurl the teeth. Use an invisible zipper foot which has two grooves that guide each row of teeth. Sew each side from the top down. The stitching will be invisible from the right side.

Business Ideas

Chapter 3 — Home Decor covers a wide range of high-value items with excellent selling potential, particularly in the custom and personalized home goods market.

Custom Bedding Sets

Mass-produced bedsheets rarely fit well or feel luxurious. Offering custom-fitted sheets made to exact mattress measurements — especially for unusual sizes like RV beds, cribs, or antique frames — fills a genuine gap in the market. Pair fitted sheets with matching envelope pillowcases and bolster covers for a complete bedding set. Offer them in premium fabrics like satin or Egyptian cotton to justify higher pricing.

Themed and Personalized Pillowcases

Envelope and zipper pillowcases in custom fabrics, colors, and embroidered names or initials sell extremely well as wedding, housewarming, and baby shower gifts. Offer sets of two or four for a better perceived value.

Bean Bag Chairs

Bean bag chairs are consistently popular and can be expensive to buy. By sourcing materials cost-effectively and offering customization — size, fabric, color, child-friendly prints — you can compete well against mass-market options. Stage your promotional photos thoughtfully: a bean bag with a book and blanket for readers, a colorful one in a playroom for families.

Travel Neck Pillows

These make excellent travel gifts and are always in demand. Offer them in memory foam filling for a premium version, and make matching sets with a sleep eye mask from Chapter 2.

Marketing Strategies

Home decor sells best with lifestyle photography — show your products in styled, cozy settings rather than plain backgrounds. A fitted sheet on a beautifully made bed, a bolster pillow on a sofa, a bean bag chair in a reading corner — these images attract buyers far more than product-only shots.

List on Etsy and Pinterest, which are the strongest platforms for home decor. Collaborate with interior design accounts on Instagram for exposure. Attend local home fairs and markets where buyers can touch the quality of your fabric in person.

Offer bundle deals — a complete bedroom set of fitted sheet, two pillowcases, and a bolster cover at a package price encourages larger orders and higher average spending.

Chapter 4
Bags

Tote Bag

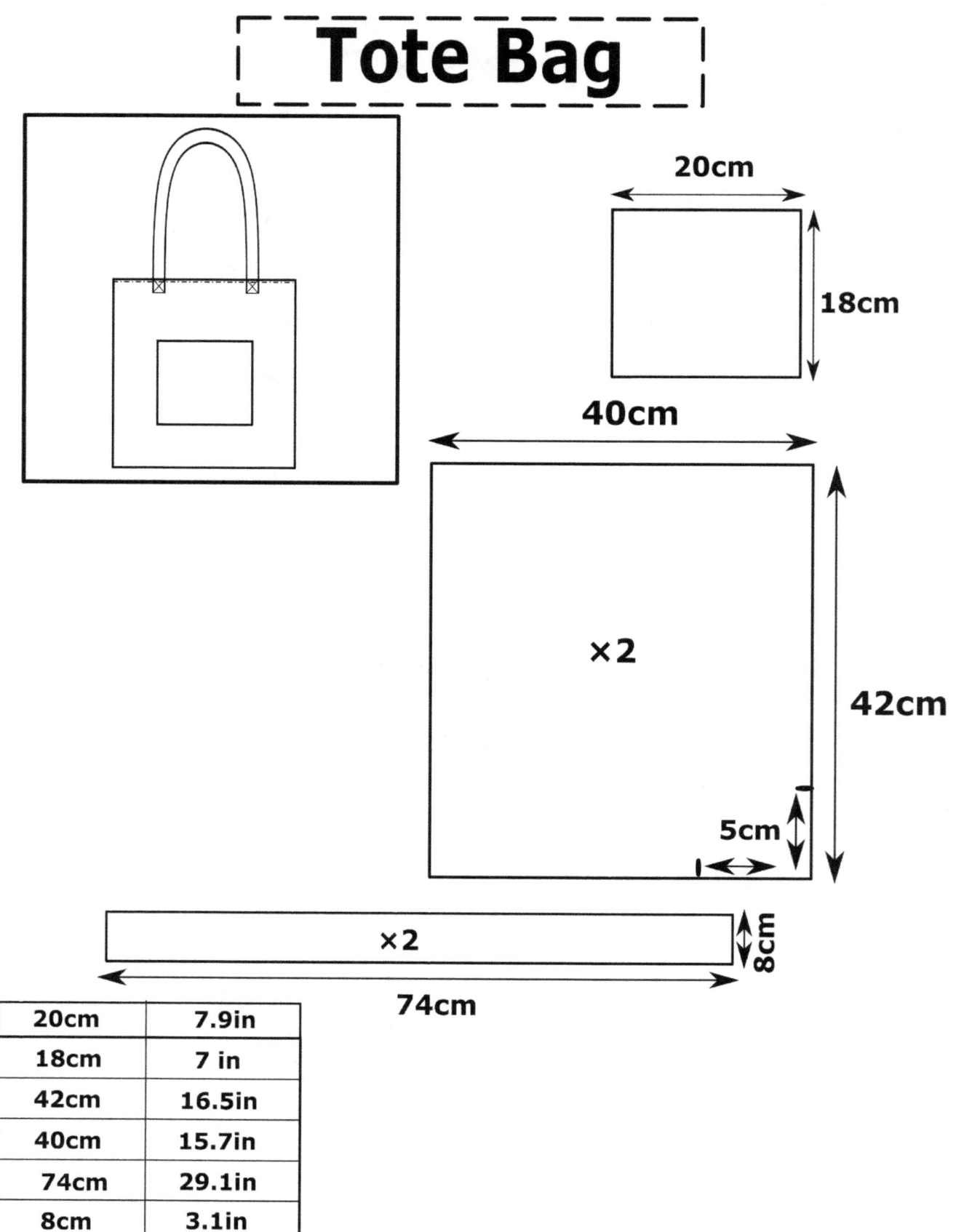

20cm	7.9in
18cm	7 in
42cm	16.5in
40cm	15.7in
74cm	29.1in
8cm	3.1in

Tote Bag

A sturdy everyday bag with box corners, a front pocket, and two handles. Use canvas, denim, or any medium-to-heavy fabric.

Materials Needed:
- Canvas or sturdy fabric
- Lining fabric
- Chalk
- Ruler
- Pins
- Scissors

Instructions:

Step 1: Cut two main body rectangles (40 cm × 42 cm) and two matching lining pieces the same size. Cut two strap strips (74 cm × 8 cm). Cut one pocket piece (20 cm × 18 cm). On the bottom corners of each main body piece and lining piece, mark a 5 cm × 5 cm square — this is your box corner guide.

Step 2: Take your pocket piece and fold all four edges inward by 1 cm and press. Sew across the top edge only to finish it. Place the pocket centered on the right side of one main body piece, about 8 cm from the top. Pin it in place and topstitch along the left, right, and bottom edges to attach it. Leave the top open.

Step 3: Take both main body pieces and place them right sides together. Sew along both side edges and the bottom edge with a 1 cm seam. Leave the top open. Do the same with the two lining pieces, but leave an 8 cm gap unsewn along the bottom edge — you will use this gap to turn the bag right side out later.

Step 4: To create box corners on the main body: pinch one bottom corner so the side seam aligns directly on top of the bottom seam, forming a triangle point. Flatten this triangle and draw a straight line across it using your 5 cm mark as a guide — the line should be 10 cm wide. Sew straight across this line then trim the excess fabric 1 cm beyond the stitch. Repeat for all four corners on both the main body and the lining.

Step 5: Turn the main body right side out. Leave the lining inside out. Place the main body inside the lining so that their right sides are facing each other. Align the top raw edges and pin them together. Sew all the way around the top edge with a 1 cm seam.

Step 6: Pull the main body through the gap in the lining bottom to turn everything right side out. Push the lining down into the bag. Close the gap in the lining using a topstitch or invisible stitch. Topstitch all the way around the top edge of the bag for a clean finish.

Step 7: Take one strap strip. Fold all four edges inward by 1 cm and press. Fold the strip in half lengthwise and press again. Topstitch along both long sides. Repeat for the second strap.

Step 8: Place one strap on the outside of the bag, about 7 cm from each side seam. Pin both ends of the strap to the bag with the strap ends pointing downward. Sew a small square around each end and then sew an X inside the square — this reinforces the attachment and prevents the strap from tearing off under weight. Repeat for the second strap on the back of the bag.

Note: You can add a button or zipper to the inside of your bag — sew them to the lining in Step 3 before assembling.

Toiletry bag

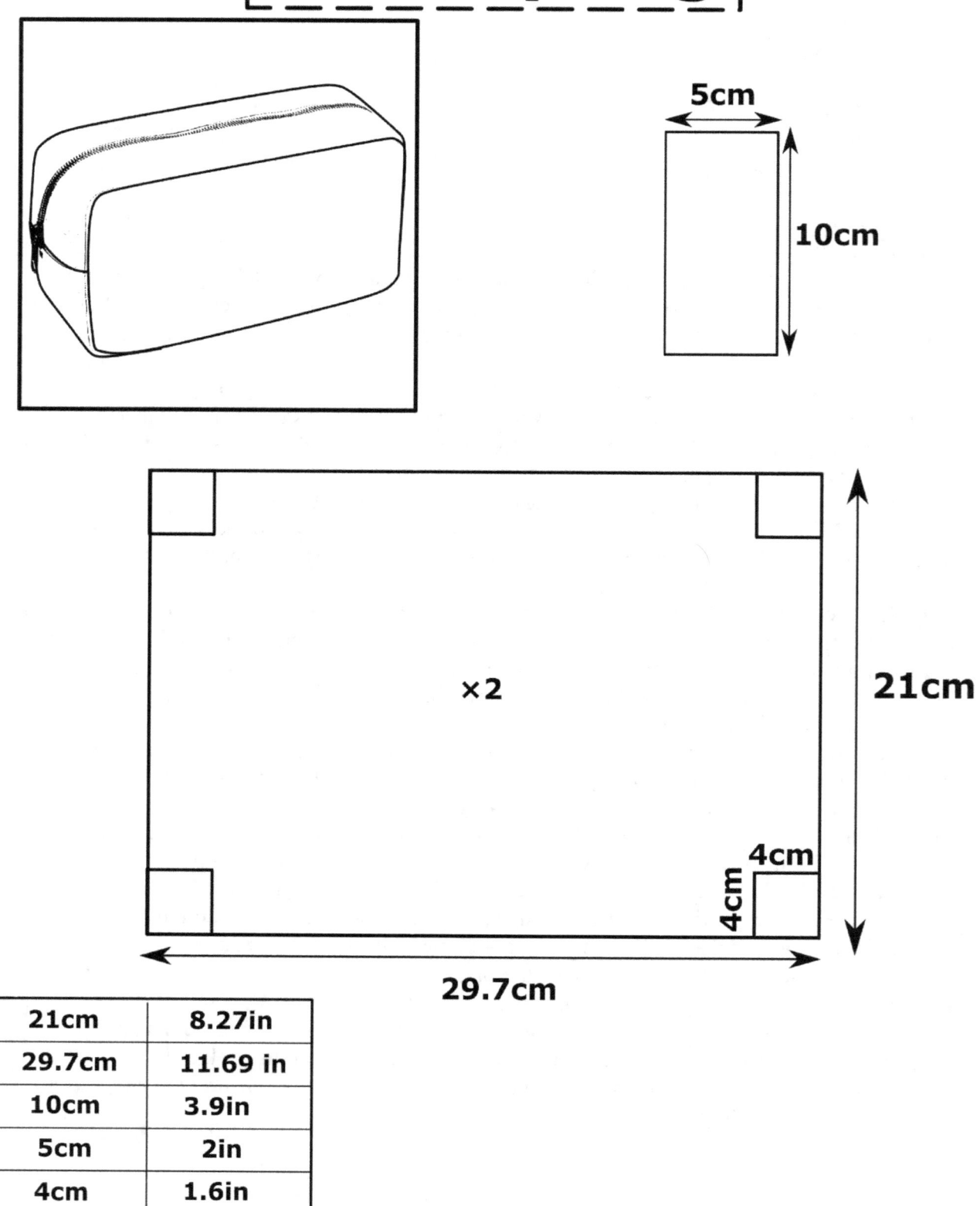

21cm	8.27in
29.7cm	11.69 in
10cm	3.9in
5cm	2in
4cm	1.6in

Toiletry Bag

A structured, quilted travel bag with box corners and a zipper closure. The 4 cm box corners give it a flat base so it stands upright.

Materials Needed:
- Fabric of your choice
- Lining fabric
- Fusible batting or wadding
- Zipper
- Chalk
- Ruler
- Pins
- Scissors

Instructions:

Step 1: Cut two main body rectangles from your fabric — each the size of an A4 sheet of paper (29.7 cm × 21 cm). Cut two matching pieces from your lining fabric. Cut one small strip of fabric that is 10 cm × 5 cm for the hanging loop.

Step 2: Cut two pieces of fusible batting the same size as your main body pieces. Iron one batting piece onto the wrong side of each fabric piece — press firmly to bond them. If you don't have fusible batting, pin regular batting to the wrong side instead.

Step 3: On each quilted fabric piece, draw parallel lines across the surface and sew along them to create a quilted texture. Space the lines 2–3 cm apart or as you prefer.

Step 4: Take your hanging loop strip. Fold all four raw edges inward by 0.5 cm and press. Fold the strip in half to make a small loop and topstitch along both long sides to close it.

Step 5: Place one quilted fabric piece flat with the right side facing up. Lay your zipper face down along the top long edge, aligning the zipper tape with the raw fabric edge. Place one lining piece on top with its right side facing down — sandwiching the zipper between the fabric and lining. Sew close to the zipper teeth using your zipper foot. Flip the fabric and lining away from each other so the zipper is now visible and topstitch close to the zipper on the fabric side. Repeat this entire process with the second fabric piece and lining piece on the other side of the zipper.

Step 6: Open your assembled piece fully flat. Position it so the zipper runs horizontally across the center. Tuck the hanging loop between the lining layers at one short end, raw edges aligned with the fabric edge. With the lining sides facing each other and fabric sides facing each other, fold the piece so that the zipper sits in the middle. Sew along both short side edges through all layers — remember to unzip the zipper slightly before sewing so you can flip the bag later.

Step 7: To create box corners: on each of the four corners, pinch the corner so the side seam aligns with the bottom seam, forming a triangle. Flatten the triangle and draw a line across it 4 cm from the tip. Sew across this line, then trim the excess fabric 1 cm beyond the stitch. Repeat for all four corners.

Step 8: Turn the bag right side out through the unzipped zipper opening. Push all corners out fully and press.

Puffer Bag

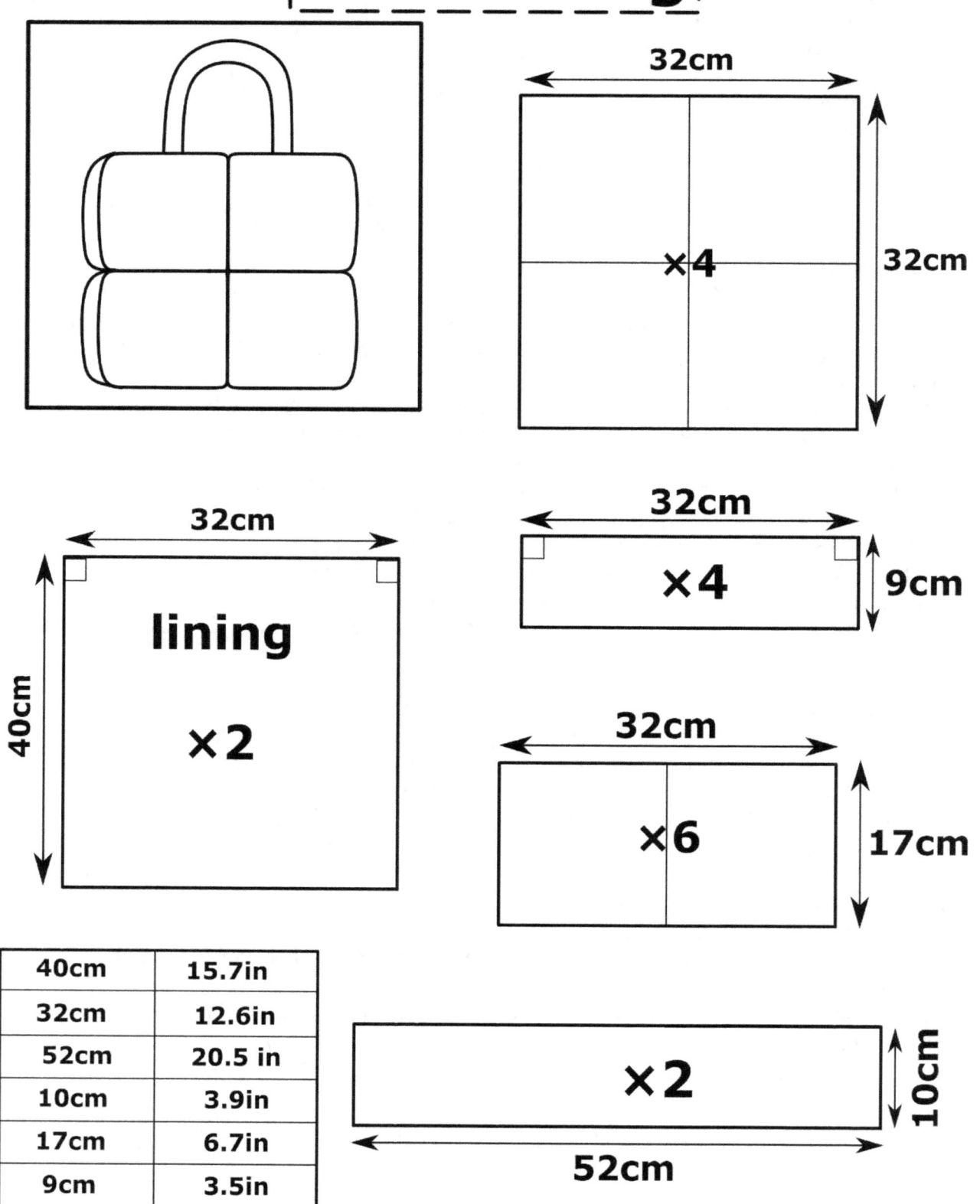

40cm	15.7in
32cm	12.6in
52cm	20.5 in
10cm	3.9in
17cm	6.7in
9cm	3.5in

Puffer Bag
A trendy quilted bag with a puffy, padded exterior. The puffed sections are created by stuffing each quilted compartment with fiberfill. This is one of the more advanced projects in the book — read all steps before starting.

Materials Needed:
- Nylon waterproof fabric (outer)
- Lining fabric
- Polyester fiberfill
- Zipper
- Snap button (optional)
- Chalk
- Ruler
- Pins
- Scissors

Instructions:

Step 1: Cut 4 outer panels (32 cm × 32 cm). On the right side of each, draw a plus sign (+) dividing it into 4 equal squares — one vertical line down the center and one horizontal line across the center. Also cut 4 side/bottom strips (32 cm × 9 cm), 6 side/bottom strips (32 cm × 17 cm), 2 lining pieces (32 cm × 40 cm), and 2 strap rectangles (52 cm × 10 cm). On the bottom right corner of each side strip, trace and cut a small 2 cm × 2 cm square notch.

Step 2: Take two outer panels. Place them together with wrong sides facing each other. Sew along both side edges and the bottom edge, leaving the top open. Then sew down the center vertical line you drew — this divides the front into two vertical columns. You now have a front panel with two pockets.

Step 3: Stuff each of the two vertical pockets with fiberfill through the top opening until they feel firm and puffy. Stop stuffing at the horizontal center line. Sew across the horizontal line to close off the bottom half. Stuff the top half of each column, then sew across the top to close it off completely. Repeat this entire process with the other two outer panels to make the back of the bag.

Step 4: Take the side/bottom strips and sew them together end to end to form one continuous strip that wraps around the bag. With right sides together, pin this strip to the outer edge of the front panel and sew all the way around. Attach the back panel to the other side of the strip the same way. You should now have a box-shaped bag. Flip it right side out so all seams are inside.

Step 5: Make the straps: take one strap rectangle, fold all four edges inward by 1 cm and press. Fold the whole strap in half lengthwise and press again. Topstitch along both long sides to close. Repeat for the second strap.

Step 6: Position one strap on the front of the bag, looping it from one top corner to the other with the ends pointing downward. Pin both strap ends to the top edge of the bag and sew a topstitch square with an X inside to secure each end firmly. Repeat on the back with the second strap.

Step 7: Take one of your zipper strips. Lay it flat with the right side up. Place the zipper teeth face down on the right side of the strip, aligning the tape edge with the long raw edge. Place the second zipper strip on top with its right side facing down — sandwiching the zipper. Sew close to the zipper teeth. Flip the strips open and topstitch close to the zipper. Repeat on the other side of the zipper with the remaining two strips. You now have a zipper unit with fabric on both sides.

Step 8: Take the two zipper-strip pieces you just made — one piece from each side of the zipper. Cross them over each other so that each piece is now paired with a piece from the opposite side. With right sides together, sew both short sides of each pair. You should now have a ring-shaped zipper panel that forms the top of the bag.

Step 9: Press all seams open. On the outer fabric panels, bring the short side seam to the center and press so the piece forms a diamond or boat shape. On the lining side, bring the seam to the back of the zipper tape. Pin everything securely and sew 1 cm from the edge all the way around both sides of the zipper ring. Optionally sew a snap button 3 cm down from the center of the zipper on the right side outer fabric.

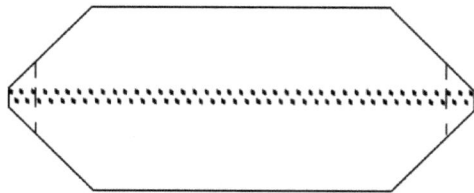

Step 10: Take your two lining pieces. With right sides together, sew the right side, left side, and bottom edges together. Leave a 10 cm gap in the bottom seam and leave the top edge completely open.

Step 11: Turn the lining right side out. Insert the outer bag (with its zipper top) down inside the lining so that right sides are facing. The zipper face should be pointing upward. Align the raw top edges of the lining with the raw edges of the zipper panel and pin all the way around. Sew all the way around the top.

Step 12: Unzip the zipper. Pull the entire bag right side out through the zipper opening. Close the gap in the lining bottom with a topstitch or invisible stitch. For the top edge you can topstitch all the way around or leave it as is.

Shoulder Bag

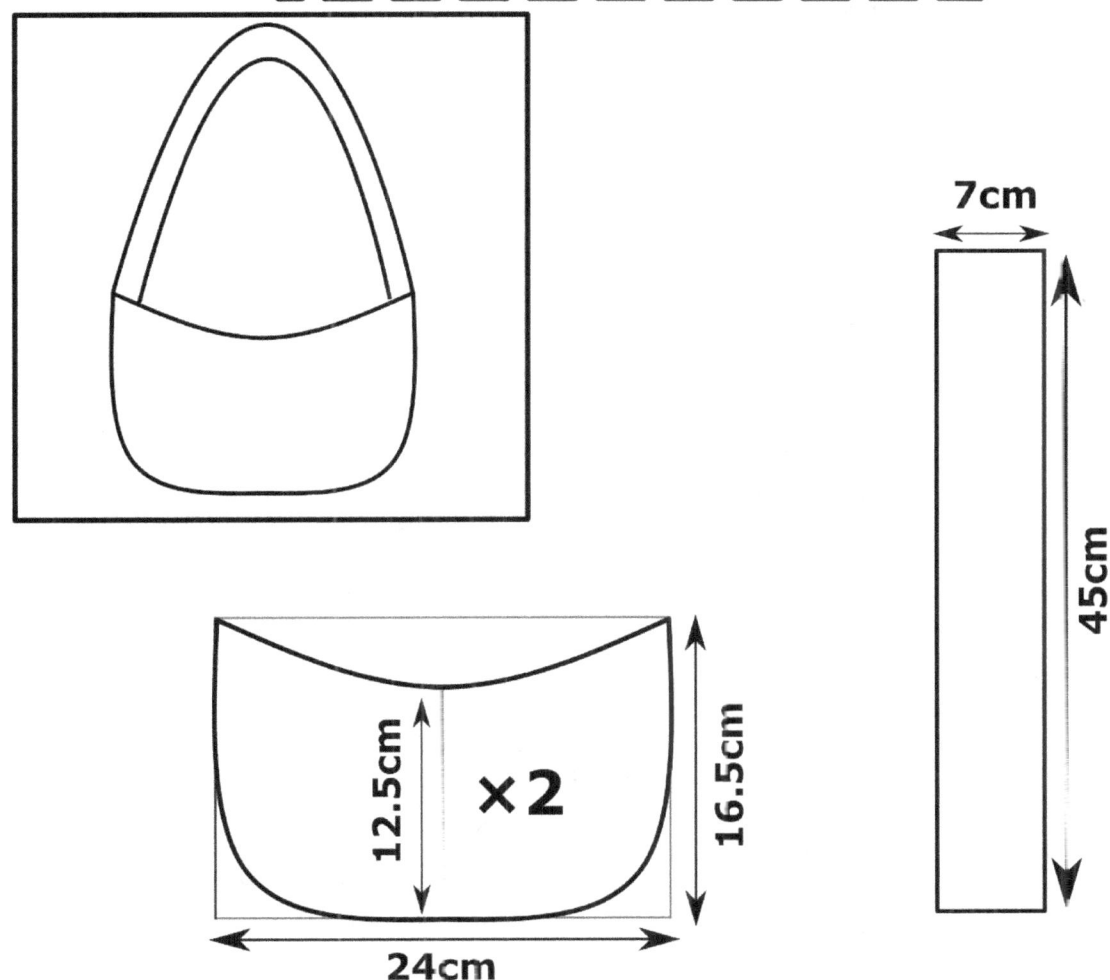

24cm	9.4in
16.5cm	6.5in
12.5cm	4.9 in
12cm	4.7in
16cm	6.3in
3.5cm	1.4in
5.5cm	2.2in
45cm	17.7in
7cm	2.7in

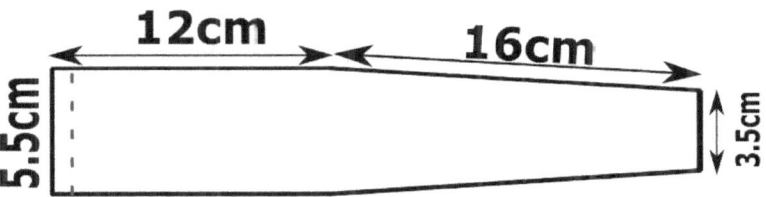

Shoulder Bag

A crescent-shaped bag with a curved bottom gusset and a shoulder strap. Use denim, leather, or faux leather for a polished look. Fusible interfacing adds structure — skip it only if your fabric is already thick.

Materials Needed:
- Fabric (denim or leather recommended)
- Lining fabric
- Fusible interfacing
- Zipper
- Chalk
- Ruler
- Pins
- Scissors

Instructions:

Step 1: Using the diagram on the facing page as your guide, draft your pattern on paper. Place it on your fabric with the straight dashed line on the fold of the fabric — this gives you a symmetrical piece when unfolded. Cut through the fold to get one complete main body piece that is approximately 86 cm wide when open. Cut two of these — one for the exterior and one for the lining. Cut one gusset/bottom piece and one strap rectangle (7 cm × 45 cm). Repeat the cutting for your interfacing.

Step 2: Iron the fusible interfacing onto the wrong side of all exterior fabric pieces.

Step 3: Take the two main body exterior pieces. With right sides together, sew along the curved sides and bottom edge using a 1 cm seam — following the contour of the bag shape. Leave the top opening unsewn. Repeat the same process for the lining pieces, but leave a 10 cm opening on the bottom edge of the lining for turning later.

Step 4: Pull the zipper slider down halfway. Take one side of the zipper and, with its teeth facing the right side of the fabric, sew it along the top opening of the exterior bag. Repeat on the other side of the zipper and other side of the bag. Replace the zipper slider. Topstitch beside the zipper on both sides.

Step 5: Take your strap rectangle. Fold it in half lengthwise with right sides together and sew 0.5 cm from the open long edge. Turn it right side out using a loop turner and topstitch along both long sides.

Step 6: Attach each end of the strap to the sides of the exterior bag and secure with a firm topstitch.

Step 7: Insert the exterior bag inside the lining with right sides facing each other. Align the top raw edges and pin all the way around. Sew along the top edge.

Step 8: Pull the bag right side out through the opening in the lining bottom. Close the lining gap with a topstitch. Push the lining into the bag. Topstitch beside the zipper on both sides for a clean finish and to close the top edge neatly.

Bottle Bag

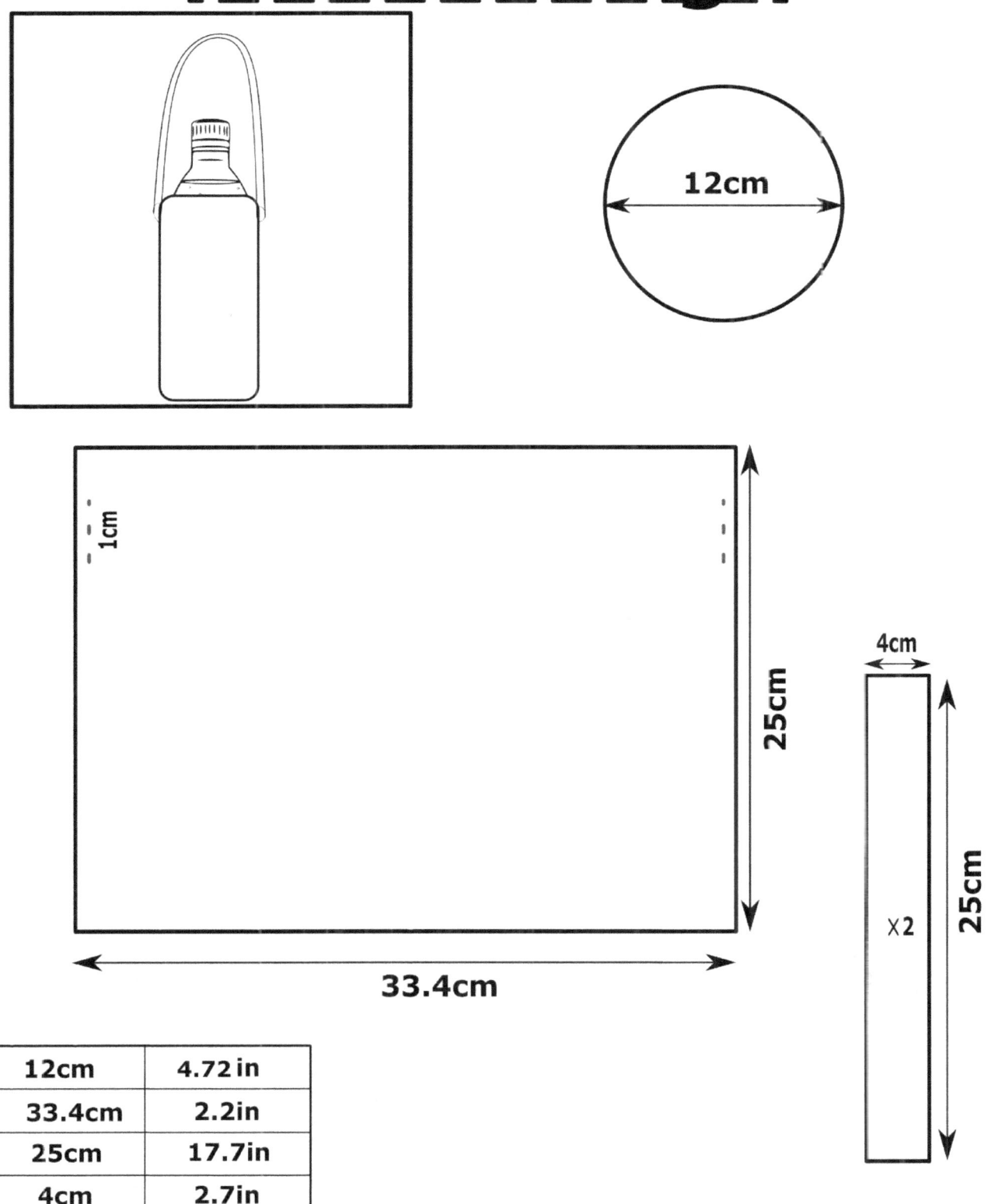

12cm	4.72 in
33.4cm	2.2 in
25cm	17.7 in
4cm	2.7 in

Bottle Bag

A cylindrical bag designed to hold a water bottle or flask. The measurements below are based on a bottle with 8.5 cm diameter and 25 cm height — adjust using the formula for any bottle size.

Materials Needed:
- Fabric of your choice
- Lining fabric
- Fusible interfacing
- Cord and cord lock
- Chalk
- Ruler
- Pins
- Scissors

How to Calculate Your Measurements:
- Circle diameter = bottle diameter + 1.5 cm (ease) + 2 cm (seam allowance) = bottle diameter + 3.5 cm
- Rectangle width = (bottle diameter + 1.5 cm) × 3.14 + 2 cm seam allowance
- Rectangle height = bottle height + 2 cm seam allowance

Example for an 8.5 cm diameter, 25 cm tall bottle:
- *Circle diameter = 8.5 + 3.5 = 12 cm*
- *Rectangle width = (8.5 + 1.5) × 3.14 + 2 = 33.4 cm*
- *Rectangle height = 25 + 2 = 27 cm (shown as 25 cm in diagram — add 2 cm for seam allowance)*

Instructions:

Step 1: Cut one circle (12 cm diameter) and one rectangle (33.4 cm × 25 cm) from your fabric. Cut matching pieces from your lining. The dashed lines at the top corners of the rectangle in the diagram mark where to leave a gap unsewn later — mark these 1 cm from each top corner.

Step 2: For the strap, cut two rectangles each 25 cm × 4 cm. Press all four edges of each inward by 1 cm. Place one on top of the other wrong sides together and topstitch along all sides. This gives you one flat double-layered strap.

Step 3: Fold your main fabric rectangle in half with right sides together to form a tube. Sew along the long edge with a 1 cm seam, leaving the 1 cm gaps at each top corner unsewn — these gaps are where the drawstring cord will pass through. Turn the tube right side out.

Step 4: With right sides together, pin the circle to the bottom opening of the tube. Sew all the way around with a 1 cm seam. Repeat for the lining.

Step 5: Place the strap on the outside of the fabric bag, positioning each end on opposite sides of the bag at the top edge. Pin them in place with the strap ends pointing downward and stitch securely.

Step 6: Insert the fabric bag inside the lining with right sides facing each other. Align the top raw edges and sew all the way around, leaving a small 5 cm gap unsewn. Pull the bag right side out through the gap. Tuck the gap edges inward and topstitch all the way around the top edge to close.

Step 7: Measure 1 cm down from the top edge of the bag and sew a complete circle all the way around — this creates the top channel for the drawstring cord.

Step 8: Thread your cord through the gap on one side of the seam, through the channel, and out the gap on the other side. Thread both ends through a cord lock and knot them to prevent fraying.

Lunch Bag

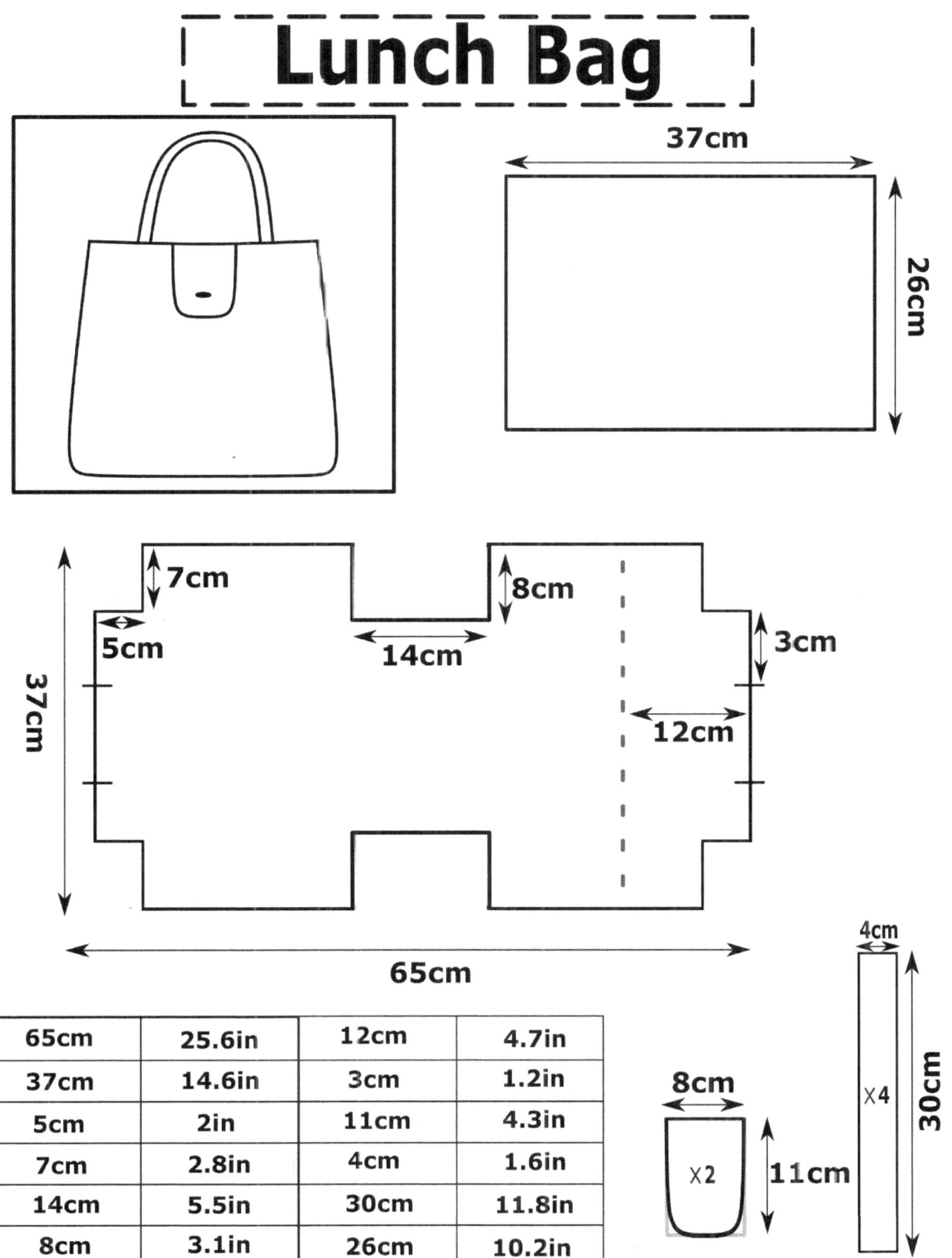

65cm	25.6in	12cm	4.7in
37cm	14.6in	3cm	1.2in
5cm	2in	11cm	4.3in
7cm	2.8in	4cm	1.6in
14cm	5.5in	30cm	11.8in
8cm	3.1in	26cm	10.2in

Lunch Bag

A structured tote-style lunch bag with inner pockets, two handles, a flap closure, Velcro, and a snap button. The main body is cut from one large cross-shaped piece that folds into a box. Read all steps before starting.

Materials Needed:
- Fabric of your choice
- Lining fabric
- Fusible interfacing
- Velcro (20 cm)
- Snap button
- Chalk
- Ruler
- Pins
- Scissors

Instructions:

Step 1: Using the pattern diagram on the facing page, place it on your 65 cm × 37 cm fabric and cut out the cross shape — this one piece will fold into the entire body of the bag. Repeat for the lining. Fuse interfacing to the wrong side of the outer fabric piece for structure.

Step 2: Cut one lining pocket panel (37 cm × 26 cm). Cut two closure flap pieces (8 cm × 11 cm). Cut four strap rectangles (30 cm × 4 cm).

Step 3: Take the large outer fabric cross piece. Fold it in half with right sides together — the two long sides should come together. Sew both side seams with a 1 cm seam, forming the bag body.

Step 4: To create box corners: bring each side seam down to meet the bottom fold, forming a triangle at each corner. Sew across each triangle — the dashed lines in the diagram show exactly where to sew. Trim the excess fabric beyond the stitch. This gives the bag its flat, structured base.

Step 5: Make the straps: take two strap rectangles and place them on top of each other with right sides together. Sew around three sides with a 1 cm seam, leaving one short end open. Flip the strap right side out through the open end and topstitch all the way around all sides. Repeat with the other two rectangles for the second strap.

Step 6: Position both straps on the outside of the bag, 3 cm from each side seam at the top. The straps should loop from the front edge to the back edge. Pin the ends down and secure each end firmly with a topstitch square and X.

Step 7: For the inside pocket: take the lining pocket panel and fold it in half lengthwise with right sides together. Sew along the long open edge. Turn it right side out to create a flat tube and press.

Step 8: Take the main lining piece and measure 12 cm down from the top edge — mark this line. Place the pocket tube across the lining at this mark, centering it. Sew along the bottom and both sides of the pocket to attach it. To divide the pocket into two compartments, sew a straight line down the center. For three compartments, divide it into thirds and sew two lines.

Step 9: Fold and sew the lining the same way as the outer bag in Steps 3 and 4, but leave a 10 cm opening on one side seam for turning. Leave the top open.

Step 10: Make the closure flap: place the two flap pieces on top of each other with right sides together. Sew three sides leaving one short end open. Flip right side out and topstitch all the way around.

Step 11: Center the closure flap on the outside of the front of the bag between the two straps, with the open raw end aligned with the top raw edge of the bag. Pin and tack it in place.

Step 12: Insert the outer bag inside the lining with right sides facing each other. The closure flap should be sandwiched between them. Align the top raw edges and sew all the way around the top.

Step 13: Pull the bag right side out through the gap in the lining side seam. Close the gap with a topstitch. Push the lining into the bag. Topstitch all the way around the top of the bag to finish the edge neatly.

Step 14: On the inside of the bag, 1 to 2 cm below the top edge, sew one side of your 20 cm Velcro strip. Sew the other side directly opposite on the other inner wall. Attach the snap button through the center of the closure flap and the corresponding position on the front of the bag.

Business Ideas

Chapter 4 — Bags is one of the strongest chapters for selling, as handmade bags are in consistently high demand across all markets.

Personalized Tote Bags

Tote bags are among the most requested handmade items. Offer them with custom embroidery, iron-on prints, or fabric paint — names, logos, quotes, or artwork. Market them as shopping bags, beach bags, book bags, or teacher gifts. Canvas tote bags are particularly popular for back-to-school season and farmers' markets.

Toiletry and Travel Sets

Bundle the toiletry bag with a matching bottle bag and a small drawstring pouch for a complete travel set. Add a luggage tag made from the same fabric for a cohesive look. Target travelers, holiday gift buyers, and wedding guests. Selling as a set increases the order value significantly.

Lunch Bags

Target parents packing children's lunches, office workers, students, and people following meal prep or diet plans. Offer them in fun prints for kids and neutral, professional fabrics for adults. Insulated lining is a popular add-on if you want to offer a premium version.

Bottle Bags

Market to gym-goers, hikers, and parents as an eco-friendly alternative to plastic bottles bags. Bundle them with a water bottle for a gift set. They also sell well alongside the travel neck pillow from Chapter 3 as a travel pack.

Shoulder Bags

Use premium materials like faux leather, cork fabric, or high-quality denim for shoulder bags — buyers are willing to pay more for these and the perceived value is high. Offer customizable strap lengths to make them adjustable.

Puffer Bags

Puffer bags are trendy and seasonal — they sell best in autumn and winter. Use seasonal colors like burgundy, forest green, and camel. For promotional photos, style them with a matching puffer jacket to show how well they coordinate.

Marketing Tips

Bags photograph beautifully when styled — fill them with matching items, shoot them on a clean background or in a lifestyle setting, and show them being worn or carried. Video content of the making process performs particularly well on TikTok and Instagram Reels and consistently attracts new followers and buyers.

Chapter 5
Baby Accessories

Bucket Hat

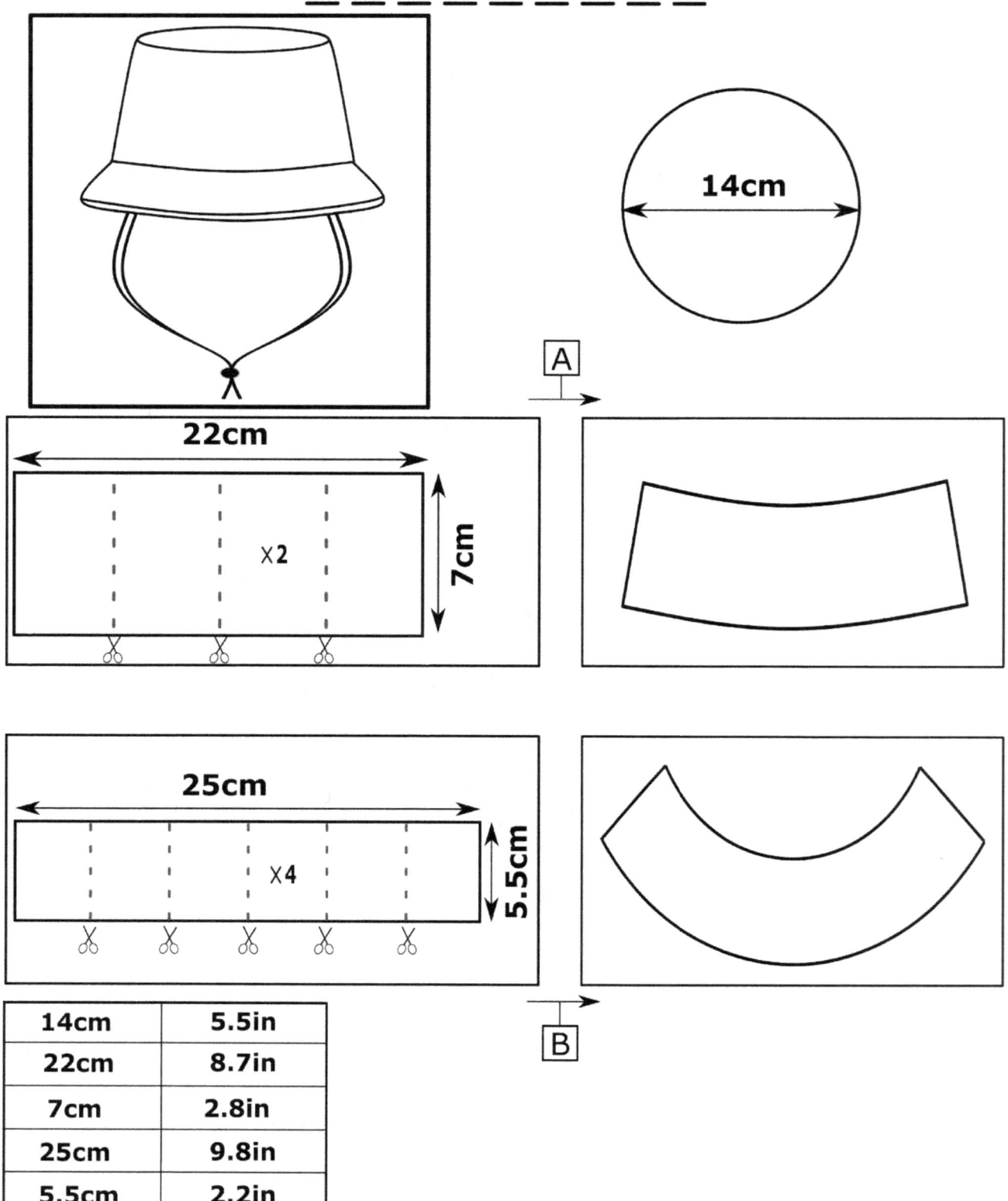

14cm	5.5in
22cm	8.7in
7cm	2.8in
25cm	9.8in
5.5cm	2.2in

Bucket Hat

An adorable reversible bucket hat with a chin strap and cord lock for safety. Sized for babies aged 9 months to 1 year. The pattern uses a clever slash-and-spread technique to create the curved brim shape.

⚠️ *Important: seam allowance is NOT included in the pattern measurements. Add 1 cm on all edges when cutting your fabric.*

Materials Needed:
- Outer fabric
- Lining fabric
- Fusible interfacing
- Bias tape (65 cm) or make your own
- Cord lock
- Chalk
- Ruler
- Pins
- Scissors

How to Calculate for a Different Head Size:

Measure around the baby's head with two fingers between the tape and the head for comfort. Divide that measurement by 3.14 to get the circle diameter. For the A shape width, divide the circumference by 2. For the B shape width, take the A shape width and add 3 cm.

Example for a 44 cm head circumference:
- *Circle diameter = 44 ÷ 3.14 = 14 cm*
- *A shape width = 44 ÷ 2 = 22 cm*
- *B shape width = 22 + 3 = 25 cm*

How to Make the Curved Shapes (A and B):

For **Shape A:** Take your rectangle (22 cm × 7 cm). Cut along the dashed vertical lines from the bottom up, stopping 0.5 cm from the top so the pieces stay connected. Leave 1 cm between each cut. Spread the bottom of each cut section outward in one direction — this creates a curved, fan-shaped piece. Trace the new spread shape onto fresh paper and cut it out cleanly. This is your Shape A (hat side panel).

For **Shape B:** Take your rectangle (25 cm × 5.5 cm). Cut along the dashed vertical lines the same way, this time leaving 2 cm between each cut. Spread and trace as before to create Shape B (the brim).

Instructions:

Step 1: Using your A and B shapes as patterns, cut the following pieces — remembering to add 1 cm seam allowance on all edges:
- 1 circle from outer fabric and 1 from lining
- 2 Shape A pieces from outer fabric and 2 from lining
- 4 Shape B pieces from outer fabric only (the brim has no lining)

Step 2: Starting with the lining: take the two lining A pieces and sew their short sides together with a 1 cm seam to form a ring. With right sides together, pin the lining circle to the top of this ring and sew all the way around. This is your lining hat.

Step 3: Make the chin strap: take your 65 cm bias tape, fold it in half lengthwise if not already folded, and topstitch along the open edge to close it into a flat strap. Thread both ends through the cord lock so the strap forms an adjustable loop.

Step 4: Sew the short sides of the two outer fabric A pieces together to form a ring. Divide both the ring and circle into 4 equal sections and mark with pins — this helps you match them evenly. With right sides together, pin the outer circle to the top of the ring, matching the quarter marks. Sew all the way around.

Step 5: Take your 4 brim B pieces and sew them together in pairs along the short sides — you should end up with 2 brim rings (one for the outer and one folded inside). Place them right sides together and sew along the outer curved edge. Clip notches along the curve, flip right side out and press. Topstitch along the outer curved edge.

Step 6: Fuse the interfacing onto the wrong side of the outer hat A pieces for structure.

Step 7: Attach the raw inner edge of the brim to the bottom raw edge of the outer hat, right sides together, sandwiching the ends of the chin strap between the brim and the hat at the side seams. Pin and sew all the way around.

Step 8: Place the outer hat (with brim attached) inside the lining hat with right sides facing each other. Align the bottom raw edges and sew all the way around, leaving a 6 cm gap unsewn.

Step 9: Pull the hat right side out through the gap. Push the lining inside the outer hat. Tuck the gap edges inward and press. Topstitch all the way around the brim attachment line and along the brim itself in 2–3 parallel rows for a structured, neat finish.

Baby Play Mat

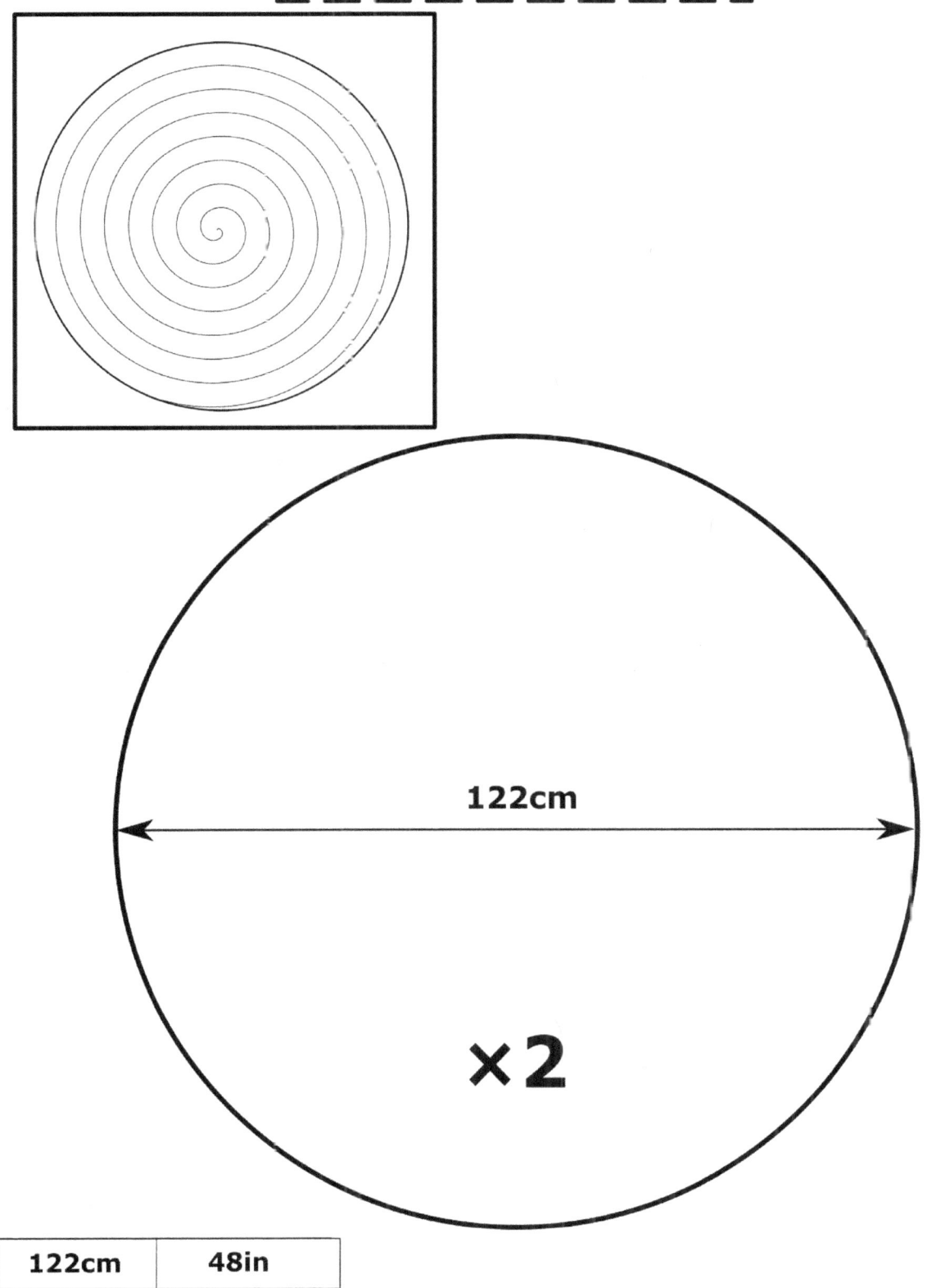

122cm	48in

Baby Play Mat

A large, soft, padded play mat for babies to lie and play on. The spiral quilting design makes it beautiful and functional at the same time.

Materials Needed:
- Fabric of your choice (soft cotton recommended)
- Wadding/batting
- Chalk
- Ruler
- Pins
- Scissors

Instructions:

Step 1: Cut 2 fabric circles each 122 cm in diameter. Cut 1 batting circle that is 120 cm in diameter — slightly smaller than the fabric so it sits neatly inside without bunching at the edges.

Step 2: Place both fabric circles on top of each other with right sides facing. Sew all the way around the edge with a 1 cm seam, leaving a large opening — at least 40 cm — along one side. This opening needs to be big enough to insert the batting through.

Step 3: Turn the mat right side out through the opening. Press the edges flat, making sure the seam lies smoothly all the way around.

Step 4: Insert the batting through the opening, smoothing it out evenly inside until it fills the entire mat without bunching. Fold the raw edges of the opening inward by 1 cm and pin closed. Topstitch all the way around the entire outer edge of the mat at 2 mm — this closes the opening and gives a clean, polished edge.

Step 5: Using chalk, draw a spiral or concentric circles on the right side of the mat — start from the center and work outward, spacing each line about 5–7 cm apart. Set your machine to a longer stitch length and topstitch along each line you drew. This quilting holds the batting in place and creates the beautiful spiral pattern shown in the diagram.

Tip: You can make the mat in any shape — square, hexagon, or any shape you like. You can also piece together fabric scraps in a patchwork design before cutting the circle for a more colorful, unique mat.

Baby Bib

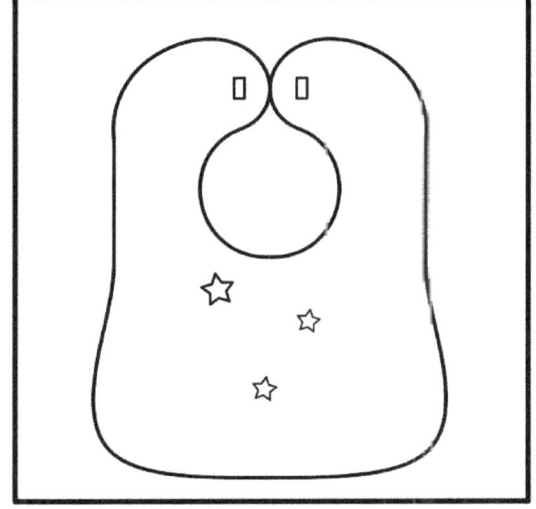

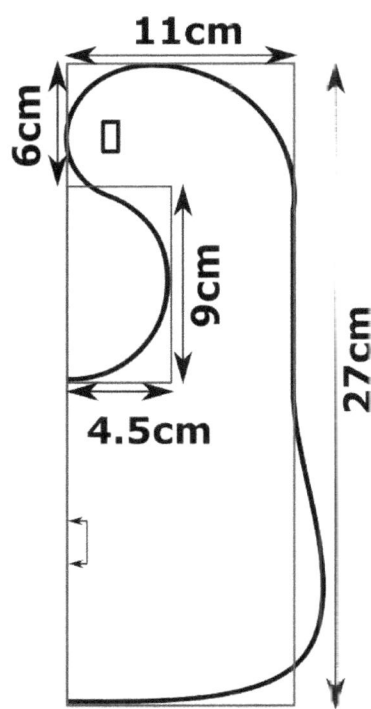

27cm	10.6in
11cm	4.3in
6cm	2.4in
9cm	3.5in
4.5cm	1.8in

Burp Cloth

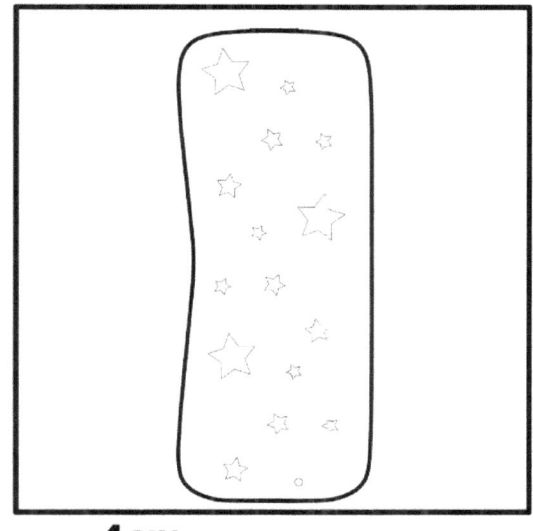

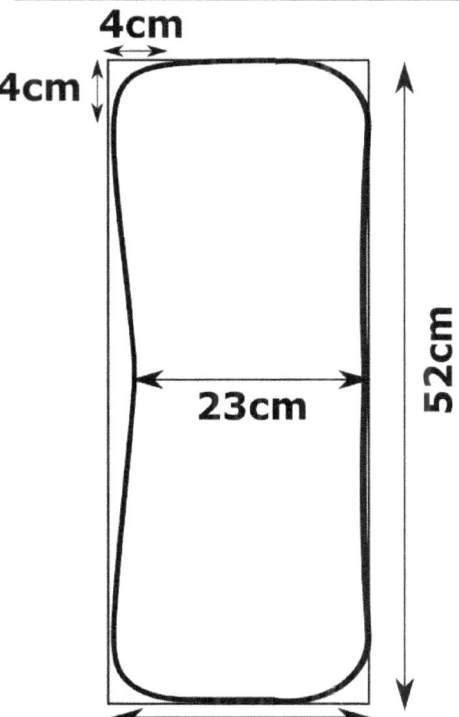

52cm	20.5in
23cm	9in
25cm	9.8in
4cm	1.6in

Baby Bib / Burp Cloth Instructions
Both projects use absorbent fabric — flannel, terry cloth, or quilting cotton work best. You can use one fabric type for both sides or mix two fabrics for a two-toned look.

Baby Bib
Materials Needed:
- Absorbent fabric (flannel or terry cloth)
- Snap button or Velcro
- Chalk
- Ruler
- Pins
- Scissors

Instructions:
Step 1: Using the diagram on the facing page as your guide, draft your bib pattern on paper. The bib is 27 cm long and 11 cm wide at its widest point, with rounded bottom corners and a 9 cm wide neck opening near the top. The neck opening curves in from both sides — the inner curve is 4.5 cm deep. Fold your fabric in half, place the pattern on the fold, and cut — when you unfold you will have one complete symmetrical bib front. Repeat to get a matching bib back. If using one fabric type, fold fabric into 4 layers and cut both pieces at once.

Step 2: Place both bib pieces on top of each other with right sides facing. Sew all the way around with a 1 cm seam, leaving a 5 cm opening along the straight bottom edge.

Step 3: Clip small notches around all the curved edges — especially around the neck curve — to help the seam lie flat when turned. Turn the bib right side out through the opening. Press well, pushing all curves out smoothly.

Step 4: Topstitch all the way around the bib 2 mm from the edge — this closes the opening and gives a clean finish. Sew a snap button or a 4 cm strip of Velcro at the back neck closure — one half on each side so the bib can be fastened and unfastened easily.

Burp Cloth
Materials Needed:
- Absorbent fabric (flannel or terry cloth)
- Chalk
- Ruler
- Pins
- Scissors

Instructions:
Step 1: Using the diagram as your guide, prepare your burp cloth pattern. The shape is a rectangle (52 cm × 25 cm) with all four corners generously rounded. Place the pattern on your fabric and cut 2 pieces. You can use the same fabric for both sides or two different fabrics.

Step 2: Place both pieces on top of each other with right sides facing. Sew all the way around with a 1 cm seam, leaving a 6 cm opening along one of the straight side edges.

Step 3: Clip notches around all four rounded corners. Turn right side out through the opening. Press flat, pushing all corners out smoothly. Topstitch all the way around 2 mm from the edge to close the opening and finish the cloth neatly.

Baby Bloomers

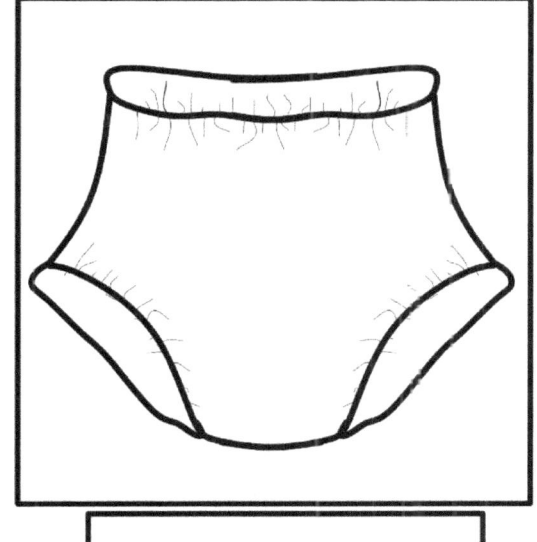

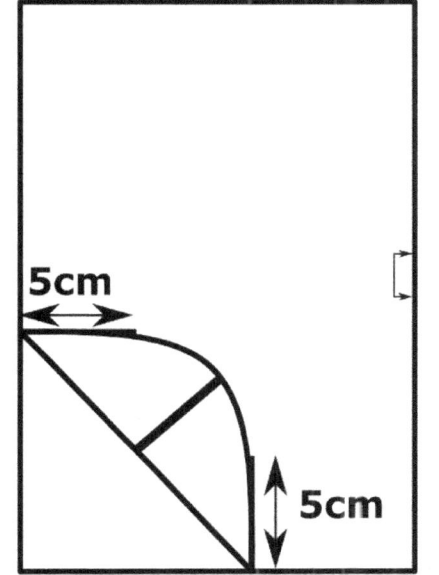

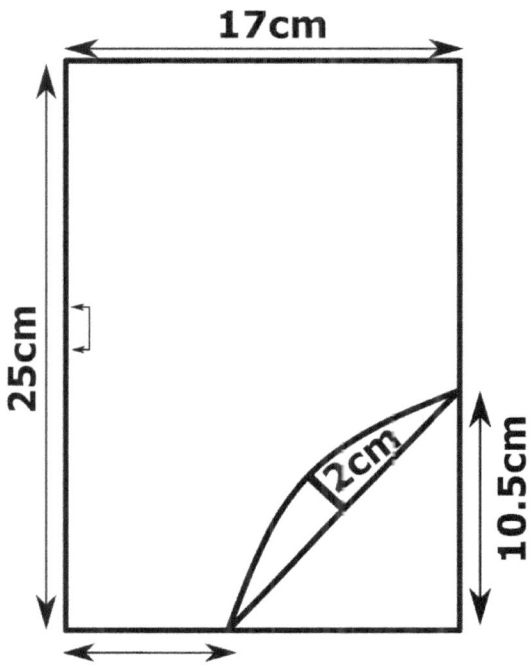

0-6	
25cm	63.5in
17cm	43in
10.5cm	26.7in
2cm	5in
5cm	12.7in
7cm	2.7in

12-24	
27.5cm	69.8in
20cm	50in
13cm	33in
2cm	5in
5cm	12.7in
7cm	2.7in

Baby Bloomers Instructions
Baby Bloomers
Soft, stretchy baby shorts with elastic at the waist and legs. Sized for 0–6 months and 12–24 months. Use lightweight fabric such as cotton, cotton muslin, or jersey knit.

Materials Needed:
- Lightweight cotton fabric
- Elastic (1 cm wide)
- Chalk
- Ruler
- Pins
- Scissors

Sizes:

Measurement	0–6 months	12–24 months
Main piece length	25 cm	27.5 cm
Main piece width	17 cm	20 cm
Leg curve depth	10.5 cm	13 cm
Waist elastic	42 cm	46 cm
Leg elastic	25 cm	28 cm

Instructions:

Step 1: Fold your fabric in half with right sides facing. Place your pattern piece on the fold — the straight edge goes on the fold. Cut through both layers. When you unfold, you have one complete bloomer piece. Repeat to get a second piece. The larger curved cutout is the front leg opening and the smaller one is the back leg opening.

Step 2: Finish the raw edges of both pieces using one of these methods: overlock with a serger machine, zigzag stitch along the edges with your sewing machine, or use the French seam method described in Step 3.

Step 3 — French Seam Method (no serger needed): Place both bloomer pieces together with the wrong sides facing each other — this is the opposite of the usual method. Sew along both side seams 4 mm from the edge. Press the seam flat. Now flip the piece inside out so the right sides are now facing each other. Press again. Sew along the same side seams again, this time 5 mm from the edge — this completely encloses the raw edges inside the seam so no fraying is possible.

Step 4: Take your leg elastic pieces. Overlap each elastic's two short ends by 1 cm and sew them together firmly to form two closed loops — one for each leg opening.

Step 5: Pin one elastic loop to the right side of one leg opening, stretching the elastic to match the fabric edge as you pin all the way around. Sew 3–4 mm from the edge while stretching the elastic — the fabric will gather slightly as you sew.

Step 6: Fold the elastic to the inside of the leg opening, rolling it over so the raw edge is completely covered. Sew close to the inner edge of the elastic all the way around while stretching it — this creates a neat rolled hem with elastic inside. Repeat for the other leg opening.

Step 7: For the waist, repeat Steps 4–6 using your waist elastic loop (42 cm for 0–6 months). The waist elastic is longer so it fits comfortably without being too tight — you can also measure around your baby's waist directly and use that measurement for a more precise fit.

Baby Sleeping Bag

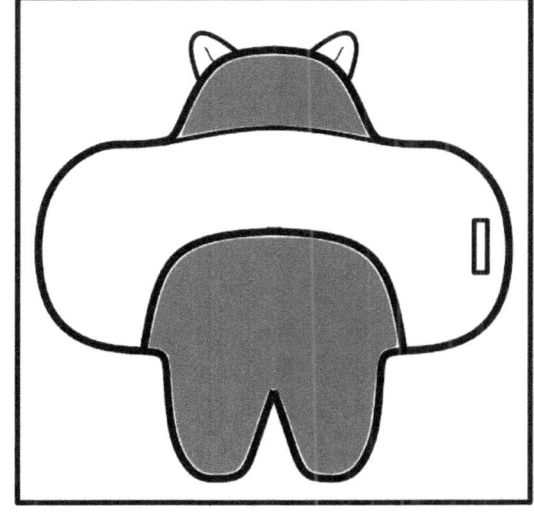
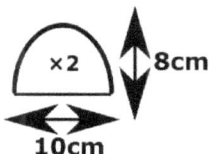
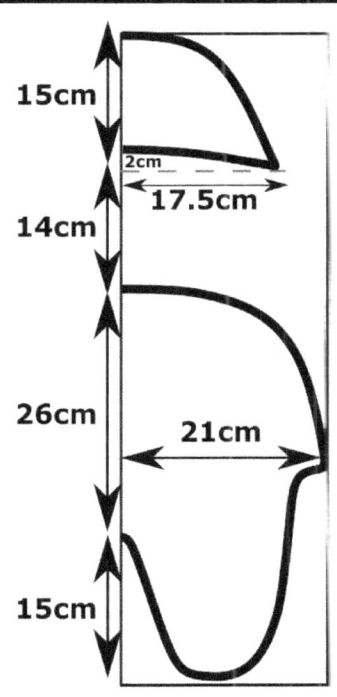
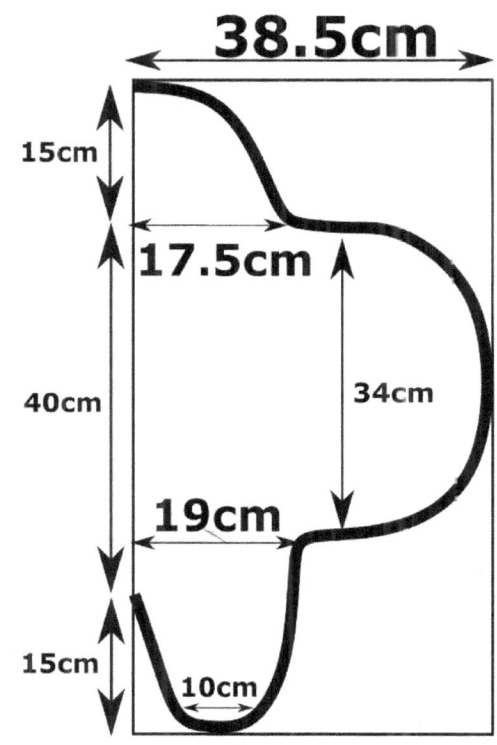

38.5cm	15.2in		34cm	13.4in
17.5cm	6.9in		21cm	8.3in
40cm	15.7in		26cm	10.2in
19cm	7.5in		8cm	3.1in
10cm	3.9in		2cm	0.8in
15cm	5.9in		14cm	5.5in

Baby Sleeping Bag Instructions
Baby Sleeping Bag

A cozy swaddle sleeping bag for newborns up to 3 months, designed with a cute bear ear hood. The bag has a Velcro or snap closure at the front. You can use two different soft fabrics to make it reversible.

Use soft felt, fleece, or cotton fabric — choose something gentle against baby's skin. Avoid synthetic fabrics that don't breathe well.

Materials Needed:
- Soft cotton or felt fabric (outer)
- Soft cotton or felt fabric (lining/inner)
- Velcro (4 cm) or snap button
- Chalk
- Ruler
- Pins
- Scissors

Instructions:

Step 1: Fold your outer fabric in half. Place the front body pattern on the fold and cut — when unfolded you have one complete symmetrical front piece. Repeat to get the back piece. Cut matching pieces from your lining fabric. For the bear ears, cut 2 ear pieces from the outer fabric and 2 from the lining fabric — 4 ear pieces total.

Step 2: After cutting, you should have: 1 outer front, 1 outer back, 1 lining front, 1 lining back, and 4 ear pieces. The front piece is the larger main body. The back piece is the hood section that wraps around the head.

Step 3: Take the outer front piece. Place the outer back (hood) piece on top of it with right sides facing, aligning them at the shoulder/neck area. Sew these two pieces together along the connecting seam. This joins the main body to the hood. Repeat with the two lining pieces.

Step 4: For each ear: take one outer ear piece and one lining ear piece and place them right sides together. Sew around the curved edge, leaving the straight bottom open. Clip the curve, flip right side out and press.

Step 5: Sew a small basting stitch across the open bottom of each ear. Pull the thread gently to create a slight curved shape at the base — this helps the ear sit naturally on the hood.

Step 6: Place the ears between the right side of the outer hood and the lining hood pieces, tucking them in at the marked ear positions with raw edges aligned outward. Pin and sew through all layers to secure them in place. Flip the hood right side out and press — the ears will pop up naturally.

Step 7: Place the outer sleeping bag assembly inside the lining assembly with right sides facing each other. Align all edges carefully and pin all the way around. Sew all the way around the outer edge, leaving a 10 cm opening along one side.

Step 8: Pull the sleeping bag right side out through the opening. Press all edges flat, pushing the corners and curves out fully. Topstitch all the way around the entire edge 2 mm from the seam to close the opening and give a neat finish.

Step 9: Sew the Velcro or snap button at the front opening of the sleeping bag — place one half on the front flap and the other on the corresponding spot on the body so the bag fastens securely.

Optional: Before cutting, you can quilt your fabric layers together first for a thicker, warmer sleeping bag.

Business Ideas

Chapter 5 — Baby Accessories has enormous selling potential. Baby products are purchased in high volumes, gifted constantly, and parents are willing to invest in quality handmade items for their newborns.

Personalized Baby Gift Sets

This is your biggest opportunity in this chapter. Bundle a bib, burp cloth, bloomers, and bucket hat together in a coordinating fabric theme — add the baby's name embroidered on the bib for a premium personalized gift. Offer these as baby shower gifts, newborn arrival gifts, or christening presents. Package them in a pretty box or drawstring bag for a gift-ready presentation.

Bucket Hats

Bucket hats sell best in spring and summer. Offer them in soft pastels, bright prints, and gender-neutral patterns. Personalized hats with embroidered names or initials are a particularly popular choice for grandparents. Consider also offering matching adult and baby hat sets for a fun family look.

Baby Bibs and Burp Cloths

Sell these as sets of 3 or 5 rather than individually — parents always need multiples. Offer them in coordinating prints for a cohesive look. Terry cloth on one side and patterned cotton on the other is a practical, popular combination.

Baby Sleeping Bags

The sleeping bag is your most premium item in this chapter. Position it as a luxury gift — use high-quality soft cotton or organic fabric and emphasize the safety and warmth benefits. Offer seasonal versions in lighter cotton for summer and fleece-lined for winter.

Baby Play Mats

Play mats are consistently in demand as parents invest heavily in stimulating baby environments. Offer them in bright, high-contrast patterns that are visually stimulating for newborns. Waterproof backing fabric is a popular upgrade option.

Marketing Strategies

Baby products market best through emotional storytelling — show the sleeping bag being used, the bib at feeding time, the play mat with a happy baby. Parents and gift buyers respond strongly to lifestyle content that shows the product in context.

Build an email list if selling online — send regular newsletters with new products, seasonal collections, and special offers to keep customers coming back.

Partner with parenting bloggers and mommy influencers for reviews in exchange for free samples. This is one of the most effective and affordable ways to reach new parents.

Participate in local baby fairs, markets, and community events where you can meet parents directly and let them touch the quality of your fabric in person. First-time parents are especially receptive to quality handmade alternatives.

About the Author

After spending several years as a teacher, I realized that while I love teaching, my true passion lies in the world of fabric and design. That realization marked the beginning of a new chapter in my life. I pursued a second degree in Fashion Design and embarked on a journey as a tailor and sewing educator. Today, I balance my work as a tailor and a freelance teacher — and this book is my way of sharing what I love most with people who are just beginning their own sewing journey. I hope it inspires you to pick up a needle and thread and create something you are proud of.

www.ingramcontent.com/pod-product-compliance
Lightning Source LLC
Chambersburg PA
CBHW062112220526
45471CB00010B/3705